F. L. Marcuse was born in Montreal, Canada, in 1916. He was educated at Strathcona Academy, Montreal, and Queen's University, Kingston, Ontario, where he took his B.A. (Psychology and Political Science) and M.A. (Psychology and Biology) degrees. In 1942 he obtained a Ph.D. in Psychology and Neurology from Cornell University, Ithaca, New York, where he was awarded the Susan Linn Sage Fellowship in 1940 and appointed to the Psychology Department in 1941, becoming Assistant Professor in 1946. He left Cornell in 1950 to go to the Washington State University, where he was appointed Associate Professor and in 1958 Professor in the Department of Psychology. He is a member of the American Psychological Association, the American Association for the Advancement of Science, the British Society of Medical Hypnotists, the American Academy of Psychotherapists, Fellow of the International Society for Clinical and Experimental Hypnosis, United States Division, and president of their Board of Professional Examiners. He is past president of Washington State Psychological Association. He has written many articles in scientific journals on psychology, hypnosis, and allied subjects, and has edited two books, *Areas of Psychology* and *Hypnosis throughout the World*. He is married and has four children.

In 1972, after thirty-two years in the United States, the author described himself as 'fleeing from behind the dollar curtain, the land of the fee and the home of the knave, and returning to Canada'. He is now a professor of psychology at the University of Manitoba, Canada. In 1973 he was elected president of the Manitoba Hypnosis Society.

F. L. MARCUSE

HYPNOSIS

FACT AND FICTION

PENGUIN BOOKS

Penguin Books Ltd, Harmondsworth, Middlesex, England
Penguin Books, 625 Madison Avenue, New York, New York 10022, U.S.A.
Penguin Books Australia Ltd, Ringwood, Victoria, Australia
Penguin Books Canada Ltd, 2801 John Street, Markham, Ontario, Canada L3R 1B4
Penguin Books (N.Z.) Ltd, 182–190 Wairau Road, Auckland 10, New Zealand

—

First published 1959
Reprinted 1961, 1963, 1964, 1966, 1968, 1970, 1971, 1974, 1976, 1977

—

Copyright © F. L. Marcuse, 1959
All rights reserved

—

Made and printed in Great Britain by
Hazell Watson & Viney Ltd,
Aylesbury, Bucks
Set in Linotype Times

CONTENTS

EDITORIAL FOREWORD

EVERY science in the course of its development has to shake itself free from entanglements, not only with magic and superstition but also with the arts and crafts of the charlatan. This is exceptionally the case with Psychology in nearly all its branches. If a case were to be made for the inclusion of this subject in the curricula of schools, it might well be based upon the need to provide every boy and girl, as part of a liberal education, with the essential critical equipment for distinguishing the Sense from the Nonsense in Psychology and its Uses from its Abuses. In other volumes in this series, Professor Hans Eysenck has set out to do this in a comprehensive way.

There are some special topics in which the sifting of the grain from the chaff has to be carried out in rather more detail; as has been done, for example, by Ian Hunter in his *Memory – Facts and Fallacies*. In the volume which this Foreword introduces, the good work is carried forward in another important special field of research – the scientific study of hypnosis.

It is part of the essential critical intellectual equipment of those who have received a liberal education to ask, on reading a book or hearing a lecture – more especially on a subject such as hypnosis – three pertinent questions: Who is the person who writes or lectures? What is his general scientific background and standing? What is his relevant first-hand experience? In the case of the author of this book, these pertinent questions can be briefly answered as follows:

F. L. Marcuse, the author of this book, has the credentials required for his important assignment. He obtained his basic scientific education in psychology through the course for the Bachelor's and Master's degree at Queen's University at Kingston, Canada, and his doctorial degree at Cornell University in the United States. He is now a Professor of Psychology at Washington State University, Pullman, U.S.A., a Member of the American Psychological Association, President of the Washington State Psychological Association, and a member of the American Academy of Psychotherapists. In addition to writing two books of his own and some seventy papers in the reputable journals of Psychology, he has contributed as an expert special chapters on hypnosis to other textbooks. Hypnosis has been his special subject of study for over fifteen years. He has had clinical experience in the field, and conducted experiments with about one thousand subjects. He is a Fellow of the (American) Society for Clinical and Experimental Hypnosis, was Chairman of this society's Committee on Legal and Professional Attitudes, is the Chairman of the Committee on Professional Ethics, member of the American Board of Examiners for Psychological Hypnosis, and advising editor for the Publication Society which publishes classical works on hypnosis. He is also a member of the British Society of Medical Hypnotists.

He has distilled his very considerable knowledge and experience into the present volume, which has been ingeniously planned (as explained in his Preface) in the light of a kind of 'market research'. This book has been written after an inquiry in advance of what the readers' questions are; and he has set out to answer precisely these questions. In doing so he displays one of the most reliable signs of the genuine scientist: when he does not know the answer to a question he says so straight away.

8 August 1958

C. A. MACE

'All sciences alike have descended from magic and superstition, but none has been so slow as hypnosis in shaking off the evil associations of its origin.'

C. L. HULL in *Hypnosis and Suggestibility*
Appleton-Century, New York, 1933.

PREFACE

MATERIAL for this book, whether it describes fact or fiction, has come from many sources: books, professional journals, magazines, lectures, newspaper articles, and personal experiences. The writer has also asked over a thousand persons what questions they would most like to see answered if they were to pick up a book dealing with hypnosis. That almost everyone has some interest in hypnosis is indicated by the fact that out of the thousand only five persons had no questions. Some of the questions asked were: 'Why do they hypnotize people?', 'Is it really possible to be hypnotized or is it just a trick?', 'Define hypnosis very clearly', 'Should you let people use you as a subject?', 'What is the value of hypnosis for the average person?', 'What are the modern and past uses of hypnotism?', 'Will a hypnotic state wear off eventually?', 'Is frequent hypnosis dangerous to the physical organism?', 'Can a person really float in mid-air under hypnosis?', 'Just how is a person hypnotized?', 'Can hypnosis be performed without instruments such as pendulums?', 'Is the power of hypnosis in the eyes or in an object?', 'Can a person be hypnotized over the radio or by television?', 'Does the same hypnotic method work for everybody?', 'How can you tell if someone is actually hypnotized or not?', 'What are the different stages or degrees of hypnotism?', 'Is hypnosis done completely through the power of suggestion?', 'Are you more susceptible to hypnosis after being exposed a number of times?', 'Does the person who has been hypnotized remember it afterwards?', 'Can a hypnotist exact physical evidence on a person's body through hypnosis; that is, on telling a subject he is being burned with a poker and actually using a pencil eraser, would there be a blister?', 'What are a person's feelings under hypnosis?', 'What type of person do you have to be in order to be hypnotized?', 'What is the percentage of people who can be hypnotized?', 'Why isn't it possible to hypnotize everybody?', 'Are those who can be hypnotized stable-minded people or just those who can be talked into anything?', 'Which is the easiest to hypnotize, an intelligent man or a relatively stupid man?', 'Can a person under hypnosis actually recall events which occurred when he was one year old or even younger?', 'Is it possible to take a person back before the time of his birth (reincarnation)?', 'What kind of person must the hypnotist be?', 'How can a person accomplish things he can never do in everyday situations?', 'Can the bodily actions be influenced by hypnosis – can a person be made to run faster than he normally could?', 'Can you hypnotize a person against his will?', 'When the person is under the hypnosis, would he do anything that he would not do in an ordinary state?', 'Are hypnotic states induced by drugs similar to those induced mechanically?', 'Has hypnosis been of medical aid to civilization, such as in dentistry, childbirth, medicine, surgery, etc?', 'Is there a therapeutic lasting effect – after hypnosis does the patient retain the effect desired?', 'Why should or should not the novice attempt hypnosis?', 'What about mental telepathy?', 'Illustrate examples of phony hypnotizing as compared to correct and useful procedures', 'What are the different classes of animals that can be hypnotized?', 'Could it be used on criminal suspects to uncover lies?', 'Can hypnotism be an aid in learning?', 'How about self-hypnosis, is it possible?', 'Is hypnosis at all comparable to sleep?', 'What nerves are affected by hypnosis?', 'How does the process affect the brain?', 'How can the person who wants hypnosis used on him go about getting it and being sure the hypnotizer is reliable and well trained?', etc.

In addition, some dozen individuals well-known and experienced in the field of hypnosis were asked what problems, if any, they considered were generally ignored and were therefore important to mention in this book. Mentioned were: the problem of attitudes both professional and nonprofessional, the question of dangers, the possible difficulty of dehypnotization, the tie-up with everyday experience, the risk involved in self-hypnosis, the quacks in the field. Finally, in regard to its use in a therapeutic (curative) setting, the President of the American Society for Clinical and Experimental Hypnosis stated: 'Just as surgical conditions are treated not by anaesthesia but under anaesthesia, so psychiatric or psychological matters are treated not by hypnosis, but the process is aided and facilitated by means of hypnosis.'

It was partly around such questions, raised by non-professionals and professionals alike, that the present book was written.

It was the writer's decision, considering the purpose of this book, to mention as few names as possible, for the book is intended to deal with the field of hypnosis rather than with individuals and their contributions. Clearly, however, the writer is indebted to many many individuals who have worked in this field, both in the United States and in other countries; for its use is international and research work has been reported in such countries as Austria, Australia, Canada, Denmark, England, Finland, France, Germany, Holland, Hungary,

12

Ireland, Yugoslavia, Soviet Russia, Switzerland, United States, etc. Should the reader be interested in further pursuit of any given topic in hypnosis or in following the writer's advice to check on individuals, general references are given at the end of this book, and these in turn give further references.

In the title and throughout this book it may be noted that the term 'hypnosis' rather than 'hypnotism' has been employed. Dictionary usage, while it suggests that 'hypnosis' refers to the state produced and 'hypnotism' to the study of that state, does permit of their being used interchangeably. Preference for either term varies in different countries. It is of interest to note that the titles of two leading journals dealing with hypnotic research use the terms 'hypnotism' (British) and 'hypnosis' (American) respectively.

The book is intended both for general reading and for supplementary reading for courses in introductory psychology, psychopathology, personality, and the like. Selection of specific chapters is feasible. The aim of this book is simply to separate fiction from fact in the field of hypnosis.

I wish to thank various members of the Society for Clinical and Experimental Hypnosis for their opinions and Professor C. A. Mace for his suggestions and assistance. I am extremely grateful to Dorothy Marcuse for alleviating the symptoms of a chronic occupational illness – passive voice, pet phrases, and pedantries of various sorts. Those that remain – *mea culpa*.

Chapter I
OPENING REMARKS

TIE-UPS WITH EVERYDAY EXPERIENCE

ARE there any tie-ups between hypnotic phenomena and everyday experience which permit of some idea of the nature of hypnosis? There are. This does not mean that the two are identical; only that there appear to be certain similarities. To say that they are identical would be to assume knowledge about hypnosis that we just do not have. What are some of these tie-ups?

A person engrossed in thought may 'read' (vision) page after page of a mystery or technical book until suddenly he 'snaps out' of his preoccupation, realizes that he has 'read' a number of pages, and wonders vaguely about their content. Similarly a person absorbed in thought may 'snap out' of his preoccupation to realize that he has missed whole sections of a conversation (audition). Or, as a further example, the writer well remembers how during World War II when lemon pie, of which he was fond, was difficult to get, he was able to obtain a precious slice. On sitting down to eat it, he got into a rather heated discussion of the coming U.S. Presidential Election, during the course of which he suddenly noticed much to his horror that he had completely eaten his lemon pie with no recollection whatsoever of its taste (gustation). These phenomena seem to be analogous to, but not identical with, the blindness, deafness, or loss of taste produced in hypnosis. Other illustrations, although possibly more debatable, may be advanced. These are the reported lack of sensitivity to pain during boxing bouts, the occurrence of highway hypnosis when driving a car at night and watching the white line in the middle of the road, reactions to certain types of music, or possibly daydreaming. In all such instances there is a narrowing of attention with a resulting decrease or absence

15

of visual, auditory, gustatory, or pain perception. All of these phenomena may occur in perfectly normal individuals.

In a different context there may be a tie-up with certain types of religion. Some church services have a high content of ritualism and make use of a hypnosis-like atmosphere. Here we have a dark interior, sombre music, a fixation point (generally a cross), a monotonous and repetitious chant, meditation, and of necessity restriction of movement. All these factors, as will be described, are thought to be important in the induction of hypnosis. It is true that certain religions appeal more to the intellectual and certain religions to the emotional aspect of belief. It is in this latter group that hypnotic-like characteristics are more likely to be present. One can even observe this by listening to Sunday sermons on the radio and by noting the degree of the sing-song (up-down, slow-fast) character of the talk. It is not being suggested that the use of hypnosis is *the* factor, but that in some religions it is probably *a* factor.

In addition, hypnosis makes use of the fact that certain moods or even words have organic reactions tied in with them. Thus, the mood of fear may have associated with it such organic reactions as 'butterflies in the stomach'; shame, with the response of blushing; the sight of lemon, with salivation; and so on. Just how hypnosis utilizes such factors will be seen in the chapters which follow.

GENERAL ATTITUDES

What word or phrase comes to mind when the word 'hypnosis' is mentioned? When well over 300 university students were asked this question, one quarter replied with such negative statements as: 'bad', 'mysterious', 'scary', 'crazy', 'baloney', 'no good', 'sick', 'strange', 'uncontrolled', and 'evil eye'. The remaining three-quarters replied in a fashion that seemed neither good nor bad: 'eyes', 'psychology', 'sleep', 'concentration', 'chair', 'dream', 'brain', 'walk', and other words of a similar nature. One lone individual replied with what might be considered a favourable response; his answer to the word hypnosis was 'interesting'. In a smaller non-university group there appeared to be greater emphasis on negative aspects, such as 'trance', 'spell', 'crazy', and words of a similar kind. What does all this reflect? It reflects the fact that the general public is influenced by misinformation, half-truths, quarter-truths, near fiction, and even outright fiction about the nature of hypnosis. This situation is not surprising when one considers how the average person usually receives his first impression and knowledge about hypnosis. This information is generally obtained in the setting of a music-hall, night-club, radio programme, comic-strip, or vaudeville act whose sole intention is to entertain. Other signs of a misinformed attitude are the frequently heard phrases: 'to be hypnotized you must be gullible', 'you can't be hypnotized against your will', 'to be hypnotized is a sign of low intelligence', 'hypnosis is only of value if your disturbance is neurotic', 'the hypnotist must be concentrating on hypnotizing you', 'in hypnosis one cannot be made to act contrary to one's moral standards', and so on. The existence of such misinformed attitudes facilitates attributing to hypnosis many occurences in which hypnosis plays no part whatsoever. Thus, for example, hypnosis may be said to be the cause for such diverse events as falling off a stool in a coffee-shop, apparent pregnancies, or even still-births.

The attitude of the writer, and of many who have worked in the field, is that hypnosis has its limitations as well as its values in both the experimental and the applied areas, and that in order to know what these are the experimenter and the clinician must first be acquainted with the facts. For man is frequently hostile to and suspicious of that which he does not comprehend – in this case hypnosis. Furthermore, hypnosis appeals both to those individuals who are looking for the strange and the inexplicable and to the outright fraud. The rigid sceptic by denying the phenomena of hypnosis, the mystic by objecting to any form of scientific investigation, and the quack by his effect on the attitude of the general public, all impede progress.

Hypnosis obviously is a field in which there is much confusion and ignorance, and those interested in this area have an obligation to indicate what can and what cannot be done. It is generally agreed by investigators that the attitude of the general population towards hypnosis needs to be changed from the present rather chaotic and suspicious one to one that is more enlightened. Hypnosis should neither be oversold by the zealot nor undersold by the prejudiced if its proper function is to be assured.

FACT *AND* FICTION versus FACT *OR* FICTION

It should be noted that the present book is entitled *Hypnosis – Fact AND Fiction*, not *Hypnosis – Fact OR Fiction*. The reasons for this are many. In looking at hypnotic data, one can describe approximately three levels. At level one are experiments which seem to the untrained observer to be downright suspicious and to suggest cooperation between subject and hypnotist, or at least pretending or shamming. At level two are experiments which seem just plain confusing. Finally at level three are experiments which are impressive and, to many, awesome.

What experiments exemplify these different levels? At level one are experiments in which, for instance, an individual under hypnosis is unable to rise from the chair in which he is sitting; or those in which he experiences positive hallucinations, such as the presence of a cat, or negative hallucinations to the effect that it will be impossible to see a given person no matter where he is in the room. It appears to the layman that such experiments are done by conscious pretending. What he generally fails to realize is that such play-acting would be difficult enough for the experienced actor to make convincing, let alone the embarrassed novice in front of an audience. If deliberate faking were present, one would expect to find exaggerations, embellishments, and a quick reaction to the suggestions given – none of which occurs in true hypnosis. At level two the data from the experiments give rise more to confusion than to suspicion. For example, an experiment which suggests to a hypnotized adult that he is now a child reveals that he still possesses certain abilities that could be possessed only by an adult (for example, defining the word 'hypochondriac'). One could quite legitimately ask whether a six-year-old child would be able to define such a word. At first

18

this looks like play-acting and rather poor play-acting at that. The situation is then further complicated by the discovery that this same hypnotized adult now possesses certain reflexes found only in early childhood! At level three, one finds data which are quite convincing of the reality of hypnosis. Here one finds such measurable physiological responses as lack of sensitivity to pain and the presence of stomach contractions, both of which react in a way which is impossible to induce in a waking state. For example, it has been reported that an individual under major surgery, with the use of hypnotic anaesthesia, lies 'like a corpse throughout'. Or again, instances have occurred where individuals in lawsuits have claimed motor or sensory damage, yet in hypnosis were able to use the paralysed limb or the defective sense organ. This does not necessarily indicate that they were consciously feigning, but shows that, in hypnosis, behaviour which is quite novel and not purposely simulated may be elicited.

The attitude of a layman or scientist to hypnosis depends on what type of experiments he is acquainted with. Familiarity only with the data from experiments present at level one (suspicion breeding) leads to *cynicism*, level two leads to *thought paralysis*, and level three to *overenthusiasm*. Being conversant with the nature of the data from experiments at all three levels leads to a sober realization of the work to be done and to *balanced judgement*.

Over the centuries as well as in recent times hypnosis has shown itself over and over again to be effective and real in myriads of ways. This is not to deny that the elements of fiction and gross deceit have often obscured this view. A recent 'victory' for hypnosis (1955) is the acknowledgement by a committee of the British Medical Association which after two years of evaluating the data produced by hypnotic therapy has concluded that hypnosis may have important applications and is an established form of treatment. That hypnosis exists has become accepted; what it is, however, is generally disputed.

Given, then, the reality of hypnosis and an attitude towards its use which neither maximizes nor minimizes, what kind of definition is possible? Before answering this question, two points must first be looked into – however lightly – namely the disagreement between different researchers and the part played by imagination.

That researchers differ among themselves is immediately obvious from reading the literature on hypnotic research. They differ on such questions as whether a person needs high intelligence to be hypnotized, whether brain waves can be altered in hypnosis, whether blisters can be produced in hypnosis, whether bleeding in tooth extraction under hypnosis can be controlled, and many other such questions. In general, one finds that most claims are met by counter-claims and most positive findings by their opposite. This unhappy state of affairs is not too surprising when one considers our relative lack of information about the nature of hypnosis. In part the conclusion so often encountered that the findings are 'questionable', are 'tentative', are 'debatable', are 'hard to evaluate', or are 'in need of confirmation' arises from differences in procedure, but stems also from the simple fact that at present there exists an area of ignorance about the nature of hypnosis. To admit this possibility indicates a certain amount of humility and a recognition of the fact that knowledge of hypnosis is not complete. To conclude otherwise would be presumptuous.

The second question asks whether hypnosis is not merely the play of imagination. If imagination can make an individual swear that he has seen and talked to a dead person, as a result of seeing faint and obscure physical cues, if it can make injections of distilled water have the effect of morphine in easing pain, if it permits painless major and minor operations to be performed, and if it can in certain cases even cause death, then the study of imagination (often hypnosis) needs investigation. To say that a patient in a mental hospital who has daily conversation with God is merely suffering from a too-vivid imagination explains nothing and is of little value. The fact that hypnotized subjects may react to a certain degree to tests of sensory and motor ability, when the absence of these abilities has been suggested, is no more an indication of the operation of imagination only than when this kind of behaviour (partial reaction) is found, as it often is, in mental patients with functional (nothing organically wrong) deafness or blindness. Such findings, it is true, represent a blow to our knowledge and often to our pride, for they do not follow the rules; to ignore them however is no solution.

All things considered, it may well be better to define 'hypnosis' by what it does rather than by what it is. For the present, we may tentatively define hypnosis as an altered state of the organism originally and usually produced by a repetition of stimuli in which suggestion (no matter how defined) is more effective than usual. Such a definition as this is admittedly ringed with if's and but's and questions of how, what, and why, and is more descriptive than explanatory. However, it is felt that at present such a lack of definitive statement is more realistic – investigation of hypnosis will not cease tomorrow at 5 p.m. Succeeding chapters will elaborate on some of the qualifications involved in the above definition.

Chapter II

YESTERDAY, TODAY, AND TOMORROW

HYPNOSIS as we know it today has in the past been called by many terms. At present we generally use the Greek word *hypnosis*, meaning sleep; a term coined by Braid in the nineteenth century which described certain, but by no means all, of the many phenomena of hypnosis. Some years later Braid recognized the shortcomings of equating hypnosis and sleep, and attempted to introduce a new name but failed. In the twentieth century it is customary to use the word hypnosis without necessarily implying that hypnosis and sleep are the same. This can be confusing, since in hypnotization and dehypnotization we do use the terms 'sleep' and 'awake', although in a different sense. An earlier term for hypnosis, and one which is still used in some circles, is 'mesmerism'.

The history of hypnosis is often popularly and professionally thought of as starting with the rather mystical work of an Austrian doctor, Anton Mesmer (1733–1815), known to some as a saint and to others as a sinner. When alive he was known to many by his vices and when dead by his virtues. He gained fame – most of it posthumously. This physician, from whose name the word mesmerism is of course derived, had in the light of today's knowledge many strange ideas. He spoke of animal magnetism (an emanating fluid, visible to some!), of universal fluids, of the proper distributions of these fluids in the healthy body, of the magnetization of inanimate material such as wood, metal, and water, of the importance of bodily stroking (passes), of the influence of the planets on man, and of many other strange and mysterious things. The efficacy of various inanimate metals to be magnetized or to produce cures varied, he claimed, from the chief of the metals, gold, to the basest, lead. This metalo-therapy had in its time many adherents.

At the same time that Mesmer wrote and spoke of these

unusual ideas he obtained some rather startling and dramatic cures. Inasmuch as such cures occurred in 'incurable' cases (so designated by traditional physicians of the time), his successes along with his unorthodox procedures did not endear him, but rather made him suspect, in the eyes of his orthodox medical brethren. Such cures occurred as a result of 'crises' that his procedure of hypnotic induction would bring about. When he had created the proper attitude on the part of the patient, he caused a crisis, with its attendant convulsive muscular twitchings and trance, to occur. After this had passed, the patient would feel limp but the malady would have lifted. Lest one think that the patients who visited Mesmer for 'nervous complaints' were grossly misled, the level of scientific knowledge characteristic of the times should be considered. In addition, it is of interest to note that a twentieth-century psychologist of considerable repute has likened this eighteenth-century practice of visiting Mesmer to the twentieth-century practice of visiting one's psychoanalyst! In his time an active state of hypnosis with convulsions was the rule, and it was only later that Mesmer accidentally came upon the passive, sleep-like hypnosis frequently described today. Mesmer's popularity being great, and the demand for his services being heavy, he devised an early form of 'group' therapy. For this purpose, he constructed what appeared to be a circular tub filled with magnetized filings. This tub had a number of projecting handles by which the patient might obtain a 'magnetic flow', usually directed to the pain areas. These handles or rods were frequently up to thirty in number and consequently that number of individuals could be magnetized simultaneously. Mesmer himself added to the gravity of the situation, not only by using appropriate music but by walking majestically around in flowing silk robes. Occasionally he would touch an individual, and by so doing he would, it was said, add to the total amount of magnetization and make the occurrence of a crisis more likely.

An investigatory committee of the French government which examined Mesmer's data verified the fact that while he actually did obtain such cures the reasons were debatable. One of his techniques was to magnetize trees and then have his patients touch them in order to be cured. But the committee discovered that many patients had touched the wrong tree; that is, they had touched one which had not been magnetized and yet were cured. Or cases were reported where people had been cured when touched by what they thought to be a nickel disc but what in actuality had turned out to be a lead disc. Therefore, this learned committee concluded, the cures were not real but merely due to the working of the individual's imagination! The obvious, that is that somehow people were being cured, was ignored and, as a result of their findings, Mesmer's reputation was harmed and he was forced to give up his practice. The committee literally and figuratively couldn't see the forest for the trees. In evaluating his work it is important to remember the century in which he lived, and the fact that he focused attention on an important aspect of therapy-suggestion, a problem with which current therapy is still grappling. It was to his credit that his interpretation of hypnosis in terms of animal magnetism, erroneous as it might be, allowed a problem which heretofore had been regarded as outside the realm of legitimate science to be investigated.

Hypnosis had, however, a long and chaotic history long before Mesmer appeared on the scene. If one is able to pierce the curtain of words which then as now obscured the problem, one finds many suggestive descriptions which in all likelihood entailed the use of hypnosis.

YESTERDAY

From time immemorial people have probably brought on some form of a self-induced hypnotic state by sitting quietly beside a murmuring stream, listening to the monotonous rhythm of a chant, staring at some bright object, or possibly at their own navels.

Around the fourth century B.C., although there are reputed to be reports as early as the thirtieth century B.C., a source of information concerning the possible early use of hypnosis was to be found in certain stone tablets now known as votive tablets. These were unearthed in Greece in the nineteenth century A.D.

24

On these stones were engraved descriptions of cures, statements of gratitude, and thanks given to the gods for the occurrence of such cures, for it was believed that they were due to divine intervention. The fourth century B.C. was the era of Aesculapius, acclaimed by many as the real father of medicine. He was thought by many to be a god and by some to be an ordinary mortal. There is little doubt from reading these early records that at that time some form of suggestion was used in a many-pronged attack upon disease. Curative techniques of the period appeared to involve massages, drugs, diet, music, bleeding, primitive surgery, worship, and suggestion. It is with the operation of this last factor that we are here concerned. In order to understand this early use of suggestion, it is necessary to try to recreate the frame of mind that many of these seekers-after-a-cure possessed. While it is admittedly precarious to try to describe in the twentieth century A.D. what the frame of mind was some twenty-five centuries ago, such a procedure is rendered more plausible because of the striking similarity of the cures described in these votive tablets to the cures which are said to occur at many holy places today.

The description of such a seeker-after-a-cure might be somewhat as follows: he or she had travelled far (in terms of time), was reverently aware of the prestige of the healing place, had seen prominently displayed testimonials concerning the cures obtained (its reputedly numerous successes may be due to the fact that anyone near death was not admitted), and further-more had not been able to obtain a cure at the hands of any previous physician. In this hope-for-cure frame of mind, the person was told to expect visions from the gods. In short, the trip to the healing temple, the admission ceremonies, the rituals, the attitude of the attendants, all had one purpose – to develop and heighten belief in what was to follow. It was in this setting that some form of suggestion, possibly hypnosis, was introduced. At some period during his stay at the healing temple the patient would usually report that he had been visited by one of the gods of health during the night, and that his ailments had been discussed, medication applied, and prescriptions suggested. Furthermore, he was enjoined to remember on the morrow all that had transpired. The recipient of such a vision was convinced that the experience was genuine and that he had been in contact with the gods. In the morning such information as he had received the evening before was interpreted for him by one of the attendants, and the suggestions given on the night of the visitation reinforced. Whether suggestion was given while the patient was fully conscious or whether some state of hypnosis was utilized is not clear. In all likelihood both were used. Regardless of which, it may be said that in one form or another suggestion was present. That human rather than divine intervention occurred is more than likely, if one considers the case of the married suppliant who petitioned the gods for offspring. She dreamt (?) of having sexual intercourse and later became with child!

In the succeeding centuries descriptions of behaviour suggestive of the use of hypnosis, though attributed to the action of the gods, are to be found in the early history and folklore of the Druids, Celts, Africans, Chinese, and peoples of almost every conceivable culture. Lest one think that these early mystical origins of hypnosis damn its use in the more recent era, it is wise to consider the beginnings of chemistry (alchemy) and astronomy (astrology).

In the more recent past – that is, in the last two hundred years – many names have been associated with hypnosis – Mesmer, Braid, Elliotson, Charcot, Freud, to mention but a few. These early investigators, all physicians, worked in the late 1700's or in the 1800's. Braid, said by many to be the real father of modern scientific hypnosis, had, in addition to coining the term hypnosis, rejected the idea of animal magnetism, stressed the role of suggestion, revived a faltering interest in hypnosis, and was flexible enough in his thinking to realize on being able to hypnotize a blind person that fatigue of the eye muscles, which he had previously thought to be an essential component in the induction of hypnosis, was not necessary. A few words may be said about Elliotson, past-president of the Royal Medical and Chirurgical Society of London. In his time Elliotson was considered radical, for he not only championed the use of hypnosis or mesmerism in medicine, but also discarded knee breeches and silk stockings

– orthodox dress for his time! It was a time when articles in such well-known medical magazines as *The Lancet* and the *Zoist* either condemned hypnosis outright or defended it staunchly. It was a time when cures obtained by hypnosis were said to be at best temporary and relapses into illness frequent. It was a time when hypnotic cures were claimed to be as good as, if not superior to, those resulting from other therapeutic techniques. It was an era of claims and counterclaims, of violent defence and vitriolic abuse. In short, it was a time when many swore by and many at the cures effected by hypnosis.

TODAY

During the last hundred years the study of and the interest in hypnosis has had its ups and downs, a cycle estimated to be between thirty and fifty years. Such cyclical interest has in the past as well as in the present been due, not to sunspots, but to a number of very concrete situations. A few of these are: the French Revolution, which caused people to be concerned with affairs other than hypnosis; the negative findings of the Mesmer investigation, which decreased the interest in animal magnetism; the advent in the 1840's of a more universally utilizable chemical anaesthetic, which made professional and non-professional people forget about the beginning interest and popularity of hypnotic anaesthesia; the rise of a mechanistic philosophy resulting from the advances made by chemistry and physics; and still more recently the need for a briefer form of therapy which stemmed from the two world wars and the inception of a National Health Service in England. In recent years hypnosis has been in one of its 'up' phases, and it is hoped, for reasons to be here presented, that it will stay there. The statement that it is in one of its 'up' phases is based on the number of professional journals dealing with the subject of hypnosis which have appeared in the last ten years, the many research and clinical papers dealing with this topic, the writing and editing of numerous books on hypnosis by competent investigators, and finally the willingness of well-known and reputable publishing houses to issue such books. All this, unfortunately, is not to say that the

27

quack or the mysterious element is no longer with us. An English film, *Svengali* (1955), catered for all the stereotypes of the occult that people associate with hypnosis; the slightly mad, dark-eyed, foreign villain (hypnotist), the glazed eyes of the beautiful but colourless girl, the eerie hypnotization across the city by means of a piano, and so on.

One should also be careful that the modern garb of today does not conceal an age-long practice. Centuries ago, the 'king's touch', or a 'laying on of hands', was thought to have extraordinary healing powers. Later this idea of the efficacy of physical contact was continued by the use of mesmeric passes, and recently (in 1956) a modern 'miracle man' instructed the members of his unseen radio audience that if they too wanted the healing spirit to come into their souls they should 'touch your radio'. In this fashion physical contact has been emphasized over the ages.

The present-day approach to hypnosis is more objective and more scientific than that characterizing the past, and this situation may result in its more permanent acceptance as a tool in both experimental and clinical work. The grandiose claims of yesterday by professional and non-professional alike concerning the effectiveness of hypnosis can only be said to reflect an ignorance of limitations and a certain degree of wishful thinking. However, innovations in any science tend to be characterized by extravagant claims. For example, it is of interest to note that Berger, the father of electro-encephalography (brain waves), believed that in the possession of knowledge about the nature of brain waves we may, in addition to adding to our knowledge of mental disease, also have the key to crime, oppression, and war. While such a claim is extravagant and has not been borne out, nevertheless measurement of brain waves has taken its due place as an important adjunct of the clinician. Likewise hypnosis, despite the extravagant claims that have been made for it, may also take its rightful place.

It is only since the 1920's that psychologists have seriously studied the problems involved in hypnosis, although historically hypnosis in one form or another has been used for many centuries by medical practitioners, mountebanks, clergymen, and

28

many others. Despite the advance in acceptance that hypnosis has made in the last decade, its study has still a rather uneasy status (a point to be subsequently elaborated on) in psychology today. Research in this area is frequently considered to be unwise, and may even be entirely prohibited. In this context it is both revealing and informative to note that Hull, a well-known American psychologist and one of the first to investigate systematically and write in relation to hypnosis (1930's), commends those researchers whom he refers to as the 'very few rash souls' who dare to defy the uneasy suspicion of the more orthodox scientists as well as that of the non-professional public.

TERMS

A very vexing problem in the present-day survey of hypnotic literature is that of terminology. Just how does this stand in the way of a person wishing to learn about hypnosis? It operates by way of discouragement. The phenomena of hypnosis are variously referred to in articles, books, and other media of communication as: 'mesmerism', 'Braidism', 'progressive relaxation' (a state which may or may not involve the use of hypnosis), 'psychosomatic sleep' (a term utilized by dentists to avoid some of the popular misconceptions associated with hypnosis), 'hypnoidal sleep' (a term referring to light hypnosis), 'somnambulism' (a term referring to deep hypnosis), 'animal hypnosis', 'animal magnetism', 'reverie', 'monoideism', 'Druidic sleep', 'mechanized suggestion', etc. The term, besides the obvious one of 'hypnosis', which is most often encountered today and which is most likely to indicate a study involving hypnosis, is 'suggestion'.

If in the search for knowledge one becomes slightly impatient at and often confused by the fact that hypnosis is buried under many terms, consider what happens when one encounters the terms 'animal hypnosis' and 'animal magnetism'. Here confusion is confounded, for the latter term involves hypnosis but does not apply to animals, while the former term does not involve hypnosis but does apply to animals! To further confound such confusion, the term 'animal hypnosis' is generally placed in quotation marks or is referred to as 'so-called' animal hypnosis (ch. XIII). What the writer is trying to show is the snarl that terminology comprises. While the question of misinterpretation and confusion about the nature of hypnosis is more than a matter of terminology, nevertheless words do comprise one aspect of the difficulty.

SPECIFIC ATTITUDES

Undaunted, it is hoped, by the confusion and profusion of terms, we may now try to obtain some impression of the attitudes of certain professional and non-professional groups towards hypnosis.

Medical. Let us start with the medical profession. It is unfortunate but, alas, true that again one finds oneself perplexed. A well-known and much-used medical dictionary defines hypnosis as follows (my comments in brackets): 'A state resembling sleep [not necessarily], induced by passes [not necessarily] before the eyes [not necessarily] or by having the subject gaze at a bright spot [not necessarily] and occurring when will power is relaxed [meaningless].' Still another medical dictionary (1950) defines hypnosis as the induction of an abnormal mental state for purposes of entertainment. Such an interpretation is completely incorrect. These definitions, if they may be so called, are misleading, and as will be shown are not in accord with the facts.

Our now desperate seeker after knowledge may next ask about the personal attitudes expressed by members of the medical profession concerning the effectiveness of hypnosis as a curative agent. He is no better off, for here again he encounters contradiction and opposing ideas. One prominent physician, formerly president of the American Medical Association, described hypnosis as being at best only of temporary value. Another equally prominent physician spoke belittlingly of individuals who speak belittlingly of the value of hypnosis! This second physician described people like the first physician as being frivolous individuals who talked without knowledge of their subject.

After reading the medical literature, one concludes that a greater understanding of the role of suggestion would be of value, for it seems that in practice some form of suggestion is

employed – be it pink pills, bedside mann
prestige. The role of such a factor, howeve
nized, nor is it being fully utilized. It woul
medical front door is shut but the back door is
Academic. What about the attitudes of our colle
sities? Here one discovers rapidly 'Why we don'
about hypnosis' (an article with this title has been
and why we so frequently have to shrug our shoul   when
asked about this or that aspect of the problem of hypnosis. In
short, the reason why there is so much ignorance about the
nature of hypnosis is simply that there has been so little research. As has already been pointed out, to work in this area, at
least in American universities, is said to court scientific disaster,
to be unwise, or is prohibited outright. Why does hypnotic research encounter such opposition? Let us take an actual incident which the writer believes to be fairly typical of the general
ignorance which exists and to give some insight into the situation. Some years ago at a large well-known American university
near the east coast a ban on the use of hypnosis was suddenly
proclaimed by the administration. Inasmuch as proper precautions had been taken, no untoward incidents had occurred, research had been going on for a number of years, the experimenters considered themselves competent, and a large number
of experimental hours were in danger of being wasted, reasons
for this ban were requested. The interview that was subsequently
granted with a top administration official revealed the following
points: there were no specific charges, but the 'well-being' of
the university was felt to be involved, there had been complaints
from the alumni (this is far from rare, for a university is likely
to hear from the alumni if they hire or fail to hire a given football
player), there was concurrence in the ban by four staff members,
which included one physician (none of whom had any knowledge of the nature of hypnosis), and it had been decided that
a hearing before a committee could not be considered. A few
weeks later an additional factor was discovered that may well
have precipitated (not caused) the ban. It seemed that a girl
volunteer for an experiment dealing with hypnosis had appeared on the wrong night. Aside from the office of an adminis-

...ial, who happened to be there on that particular ...ne building (shared by psychology and the administra-...on) was in total darkness. Unfortunately, as it turned out, the girl came to the official's office to ask for information. She simply asked where the experiment in hypnosis was being conducted. These are the bare facts, as told by the girl involved in the incident. Needless to say, the story when subsequently heard had been considerably embellished. Another general reason why research in hypnosis is often discouraged in American institutions of higher learning is the opposition of members of the medical profession. Such opposition by physicians who believe that no form of hypnosis should be practised either experimentally or clinically by psychologists, is often based on a 'feeling that', or the fact that, a patient blames his present troubles on being hypnotized some five, ten, or even fifteen years ago, or the belief that hypnosis is an area which only the medically trained should investigate. All these are points which tend to show a lack of knowledge about the nature of hypnosis. Fear of pressure from parents of students or from alumni appears to be the most frequently encountered reason for the ban on hypnotic research. Because of this, even departments that are doing research in the area of hypnosis have adopted one of the following procedures: they have used only individuals over twenty-one (thereby cutting down on the number of subjects available for experimentation), or they have requested written permission from the parents of subjects under twenty-one (thereby adding to the misconception that hypnosis is essentially dangerous), or they have used paid non-university individuals (thereby requiring financial support). Ironically enough, it was just such a paid non-university individual over twenty-one who was the only person (to the writer's knowledge) who ever sued a university for lowered efficiency alleged to have occurred as a result of being hypnotized.

If we are to progress in our attitude towards hypnosis from one of giggly apprehension to one of mature comprehension, a more serious educational appraisal is required. The attitudes and actions existing in many of our well-known universities today can only accentuate the mysterious and awesome in hypnosis. An outright or implied ban on it constitutes a disservice to legitimate research. Scientific principle and knowledge rather than expediency should be the yardstick.

Within universities it may be asked what the attitudes of psychology departments are. Here many of the points indicated in previous paragraphs are relevant. 'Don't rock the boat' and 'Let sleeping dogs lie' appear to be the unwritten rules. In psychology texts little is to be found wrong with what is said about hypnosis, for the simple reason that little is to be found! For example, of four recent popular introductory textbooks in psychology, two make no reference whatsoever to the phenomena of hypnosis, one has a passing reference some three lines in length, and one has a page discussing the problem. Unfortunately in this last book half of the one page is taken up by a dogmatic statement without supporting data concerning a highly controversial issue. In courses where the topic of hypnosis may be relevant, the average psychologist passes over this area with a few scant comments (he generally has to because of lack of knowledge), and these remarks are often incorrect. In an unpublished study conducted in the United States, it was revealed that only five of seventy-four leading universities provided study, to any significant degree, of this area of behaviour. If this is true of the psychologist and would-be psychologist who is interested – it is said – in all kinds of human behaviour, then the situation which confronts the physician and would-be physician must be described as being even more regrettable.

Religious. What is the attitude of the Catholic Church to the use of hypnosis? First it may be wondered why a particular religious group is singled out. In answer to this question, it may be said that the Catholic Church represents, in the American culture, a large group about whose attitude towards the use of hypnosis there has been considerable debate. A statement received from an individual high in the Catholic hierarchy serves as a guide. This communication said that the Holy See condemns only the improper use of hypnosis and that many of the Church's earlier restrictions were a vestige of its previous suspicions about hypnosis. It is realized by the Holy See, the communication goes on to say, that nowadays there is a proper and legitimate place for hypnosis. The only discordant and rather puzzling note in the statement is the sentence to the effect that continued subjection to hypnosis is 'morally' wrong. Exactly what 'continued' means in terms of frequency can only be guessed. The general conclusion, however, can be made that religious adherence (except possibly in certain small sects) is not an impediment to clinical or experimental hypnosis. The author has found no reference to any particular stand on hypnosis on the part of other major religious groups.

TOMORROW

If the preceding points are some of the negative or neutral ones associated with hypnosis, what then, if any, are some of the positive factors? It has been previously suggested that the study of hypnosis is on the upswing, and reasons were advanced for this belief. Justification as to why this upswing may be permanent may also lie in the existence of two important groups which are playing significant roles in the progress of hypnosis. They are the Society for Clinical and Experimental Hypnosis (United States), founded in 1949, and the British Society of Medical Hypnotists (England), established a year earlier.

The former group, with which the writer is better acquainted, consists of members who possess the medical (M.D.), doctoral (Ph.D.), or dental (D.D.S.) degree, and belong to their appropriate professional societies. In addition, they must have published in the field of hypnosis or have had at least two years' experience with its clinical use. Other areas of specialization and training experience are considered on an individual basis, and persons interested in hypnosis but not fulfilling all the above requirements may be eligible for different classes of membership. It has been said that these requirements for membership are too rigorous. Are they? When one considers both the existing negative professional attitude and the aims of the Society, which are in part to: (1) encourage research; (2) encourage writing (over fifteen books have been written by its members); (3) set up standards of competency; and (4) foster close relationships between those doing research in the field of hypnosis, then advantage needs to be taken of every possible factor including prestige. It may be argued on the basis of these facts that a select rather than a broad membership is indicated at this time. At present the membership of the Society for Clinical and Experimental Hypnosis numbers a little over three hundred, of which somewhat over half possess a medical degree, and the remainder are mainly psychologists and dentists. This Society, in addition to these broad aims, sponsors annual meetings at which scientific papers on hypnosis are read; endorses relevant legislation; has its own book, reprint, and record lending library on topics concerned with hypnosis; edits an annual review of hypnotic literature; puts out the quarterly *Journal of Clinical and Experimental Hypnosis* (circulation approximately 800); attempts to educate the public with regard to the uses and abuses of hypnosis, and provides training through its Institute for Research. (See also ch. XIII.) A person engaging in popular demonstration of hypnosis for purposes of entertainment is not eligible to join the Society, and furthermore any member who does so is required to resign. It is not intended to imply that all is sweetness and light within the Society among its members or that differences of opinion do not exist. While there is agreement on the need for further research, as well as agreement that psychologists are entitled to do experimentation in the area of hypnosis, there is far from unanimity among its members as to who should use hypnosis therapeutically. This controversy is not peculiar to the Society for Clinical and Experimental Hypnosis alone, for it parallels the objections of psychiatrists to clinical psychologists doing any type of therapeutic or curative work.

Other American professional associations with lower standards for membership admission have appeared on the scene. They emphasize application (dental and clinical) to the practical exclusion of experimentation. Such a one-sided emphasis does not bode well for obtaining answers to the many questions posed by the phenomenon of hypnosis. Such groups, it is feared, may unwittingly stress quantity rather than quality.

The British Society of Medical Hypnotists has many of the same goals as its American counterpart (Society for Clinical and Experimental Hypnosis). The role, however, of psychologists is minimized if not entirely absent by reason of the British Society's local membership requirement of being a 'fully qualified medical man'. As a consequence of this, its emphasis is mainly on the clinical side of hypnosis as reflected in the articles in its journal (*The British Journal of Medical Hypnotism*). The authors of these articles (apart from those reprinted from other countries) tend to be physicians, for the Society has little contact with English universities, and there is an absence of experimental orientation.

Are there any other beneficial signs? There are. In Soviet Russia there is said to be a large amount of serious research being done in the field of hypnosis, especially with regard to the physiological mechanisms that may be involved in the induction of hypnosis. Their attitude is one which regards hypnosis not as being essential for either clinical or experimental research, but rather as a tool which may be profitably used. In England one might point to such things as the law banning the hypnotizing of individuals under twenty-one years of age for purposes of entertainment to informal agreement by some of the prominent newspapers to refuse advertisements offering hypnotic treatment, and finally the recommendation of a committee of the British Medical Association that medical students be grounded in the subject of hypnosis. In the United States there has recently been an upsurge of interest on the part of dentists in the possible application of hypnosis, as well as a slight easing of suspicion on the part of professional and non-professional individuals. As one example, it may be mentioned that two hundred physicians and dentists turned out for a symposium on hypnosis where only forty had been expected. We might remove the word 'very' from Hull's dedication ('to the *very* few rash souls') to those who do hypnotic research.

It took some time before psychiatry was recognized as other than the stepchild of medicine. In similar fashion, it may take some time before hypnotherapy and hypnosis are as fully accepted as psychiatry and psychology. As the British and American societies for the advancement of hypnosis grow in strength, they will be able to affect desirable legislation which in turn may change for the better public and professional opinions, and this may ultimately result in more research and consequently more knowledge – in short, a benign circle may result.

Chapter III

HYPNOSIS AND SCIENCE

PROOF of hypnosis has all too often in the past relied upon the testimony of men of 'unimpeachable integrity' or rested on random observation. This kind of proof has today been largely discarded because of the fallibility of human testimony. However, one has to be careful in criticizing these early researchers in hypnotic work for not utilizing more refined methods, for to do so would be like criticizing a child for not being an adult! With present-day more rigorous techniques of scientific control, less dramatic but sounder results from hypnosis have been obtained, the data being characterized as small but significant. Despite the improvement in scientific procedure, the present-day use of case histories, while suggestive, has its drawbacks. Often the cases are few in number and without ample control, limitations which will be discussed in subsequent paragraphs.

It is of value from a scientific point of view to differentiate investigations of hypnosis proper from investigations of problems in which hypnosis plays only a part. While scientific method is common to both types of problems, such a distinction is of value in seeing the different roles of hypnosis. Study of the scientific method employed in either case allows one to judge the soundness of the conclusions reached. It has been said by some proponents as well as some opponents of hypnosis that the application of rigorous scientific controls is impossible, and because of this hypnosis can never be considered a science. Such a statement if true would have serious implications for the study of hypnosis, and its answer is important for the clinician as well as the experimentalist.

SCIENTIFIC PROCEDURE IN HYPNOSIS

In mechanical engineering the question often arises as to what type of conductor may best satisfy the requirements for conductance. In answering this question, many things must be considered: the distance apart of the steel towers that hold the electric wires, the thickness of the wires, the clamps used to hold the wires, and so on. In experimental psychology there are similar complexities, and in addition there is the fact that one is now dealing with living subjects. In clinical psychology the complexity is further increased by the fact that the subject-matter involved is abnormal psychology, a topic about which comparatively little is known. The use of hypnosis in clinical or experimental work adds still a further unknown to an already complex situation. Such circumstances do not mean giving up in despair and not attempting to utilize scientific method, but rather mean that the study of hypnosis may require a modified scientific procedure. Such a scientific procedure cannot be considered as either inferior or superior to the more traditional laboratory method – it is merely different. While we are prone to think of the laboratory method with its large numbers, control of environment, and in general its employment of rigorous procedures as being *the* scientific method, it should be realized that this procedure suffices for some problems but is not able to handle others. The study of the behaviour of animals in their natural habitat, for example the ant, or a study of the 'homing' behaviour of pigeons, requires other than traditional laboratory methods. The investigation of hypnosis similarly requires a somewhat different scientific procedure. Let us exemplify.

It has been reliably reported, photographed, and attested to by the dentists involved that with hypnotic rather than chemical anaesthesia wisdom teeth may be extracted and normally very painful cavities filled. In the performance of this, no pain or indication of pain whatsoever occurred. Now, if one were to follow in rigid fashion the traditional and usual requirements of the laboratory method in establishing the scientific validity of the above example, use of large numbers, repetition, and control would be required. How would these requirements work out in practice? With regard to the first criterion, the need for large numbers, it would obviously not be an easy matter to find many subjects who are hypnotizable, need their wisdom teeth extracted, and are willing to have them extracted with hypnotic anaesthesia. While the use of large numbers is a praiseworthy objective, because it reduces the possibility that factors unrelated to the experiment will have an effect on results, it is not always feasible or practical. Hypnosis has, however, suffered from the fact that some of its best-known and most widely quoted results have come from investigations using less than ten subjects. Repetition was said to be the second requirement, and here the question that arises is whether the repetition is to be on the same or on a different individual. If on the same individual, it may be found that a second extraction is not necessary or if a second extraction is performed it may legitimately be asked whether the depths of hypnosis on the two occasions are comparable. The question also arises as to whether the two teeth are equally embedded. If on a different individual, problems of a similar nature to the ones already described present themselves. Are the two hypnotic states in the different individuals comparable? Are the teeth equally embedded? These are all problems which arise whether one or more than one individual is involved. The third requirement is control. This if followed would require that another wisdom tooth be extracted without benefit of any anaesthetic whatsoever. Not only would it be difficult to find subjects who would volunteer for such a procedure, but it would be mandatory to have the two wisdom teeth equally embedded. The use of the control experiment or procedure, while not always feasible, is generally wise. It tries to find out whether the phenomenon (painlessness) elicited in hypnosis is peculiar to that state alone or whether it can be produced in a similar degree without hypnosis. In this way it provides a valuable check on results and leads to caution concerning conclusions when control is lacking, for it has been found that some individuals are as suggestible without hypnosis as some with hypnosis. Saying to a patient that he, the patient, would have been much worse off if he had not been treated may be correct, a shrewd guess, or face-saving. Without some sort of control, it is not always clear which situation exists.

When the use of a control group, large numbers, and repetition are not feasible, what is done in practice is not to throw scientific caution to the winds but to look up the past history of the individual. This is done to ascertain whether on other occasions when not in hypnosis the subject has shown the normal sensitivity and the usual avoidance reaction to pain. While this may not meet the rigid requirements of the laboratory experiment, it is feasible and scientifically appropriate.

A clinical situation which approximated the use of a control group was reported in the nineteenth century before chemical anaesthetics were available. The physician in charge employed hypnotic anaesthesia in a tumour operation 'without her [the patient] feeling it'. Four months later a similar operation was performed on the same patient owing to a return of the tumour. The second operation, which may be thought of as a control operation, was described as follows: 'She has been hypnotized daily but without effect. I therefore operated on her today as we could spare no more time. The poor old woman screamed miserably the full time, crying that I was murdering her; and she continued in the greatest pain for hours afterwards.' Or again 'A lady had an abscess connected with disease of the frontal bone. ... The wound was closed and opened by the lancet. She experienced so much pain on each occasion that it induced me to hypnotize her; afterwards she made no complaint. ... On one occasion I was anxious to ascertain how she would feel by operating *without hypnotizing*, when the result was so distressing that it induced me always in the future to hypnotize her before such operations, and then all went on well.'

The question of the representativeness of the samples from which conclusions are drawn about the nature of hypnosis may be raised, especially with regard to dental patients and experimental volunteers who make up the bulk of research subjects. In the former case there is evidence that the sample is biased in favour of the higher socio-economic groups (ch. X), who can afford dental work. In the latter case the same finding exists, for most of the subjects are university students; but, in addition, it may be asked whether within this group volunteers for hypnotic experiment differ from non-volunteers. Are such volunteers emotionally stable? Are they submissive? Are they stupid? Are they exhibitionists? These are but some of the questions that are frequently brought up. Results of research seem to indicate otherwise (cf. ch. VI).

Comparison of results obtained from experimental volunteers for hypnotic experiments and patients for hypnotherapy must be cautiously made, for the samples vary considerably. They differ significantly in their expectations (curiosity versus cure), in the situation they encounter (laboratory versus consulting-room), and in the degree of emphasis placed on hypnotic induction (the experimental attitude that one subject is as good as another and can be replaced by another versus the clinical attitude of the need to hypnotize a specific patient).

Instrumentation is also important in science, for just as it would obviously be foolish to enter a speed-car race with a 1910 model, so too would it be incorrect to use insensitive instruments in hypnotic research. Hypnotically induced deafness is said to produce a complete loss of startle reaction. This appears to be true as far as can be detected by the human eye. But sensitive instruments reveal that some reaction to sound is occurring. The amount of reaction was found to be more than is present in known organic deafness, but significantly less than is present in controls (that is, in individuals who are consciously and deliberately trying to simulate organic deafness).

SOME NEGATIVE CASES

Hypnotic research has frequently failed to utilize proper scientific precautions, and has, as a consequence, reached some conclusions illegitimately; especially, one suspects, in reports of some hundred years ago.

It may be found that producing hypnosis by induction procedure A yields poor results, while induction procedure B yields excellent results. The conclusion that procedure B is therefore superior to procedure A is unwarranted, for procedure B was used on the second occasion while procedure A was used only on the first attempt. Practice effects were not taken into account. In another experiment an individual was brought back (regressed) in his life's span five, ten, and fifteen years, and asked what day of the week his birthday fell on in that particular year. By blind chance alone he would be right in one of seven replies;

in short his birthday had to fall on one of seven name days (Monday, Tuesday, etc.), consequently it is against this chance number of one in seven that the obtained results must be compared, not with zero, as was done. The day of the week on which Christmas fell in the regressed year was also asked. Response to this question may well be tied to the first question and makes evaluation of results difficult. For example, the writer's birthday is on 4 December, being exactly three weeks from 25 December; the name-day of the week for both Christmas and his birthday are the same. Such a fact should be taken into account in evaluating results. One is also not quite sure whether reports of success and failure were given to the subjects – information which would affect chance. Despite these various objections to the procedure, the data still indicate significance, but also indicate the use of a rather careless experimental design. Simple and straightforward as the above points seem to be, they are often ignored.

A logical fallacy often present in hypnotic work is to reason from the facts obtained from the group back to an explanation of the same facts obtained from the original group. There is no inherent objection to such reasoning after the facts *if* such reasoning is used to predict results on *new* groups. The French have a saying *'savoir c'est prévoir'* – to know is to predict – an important feature of science. For example, if it is found that all redheads in a certain group are hypnotizable, one might tentatively make a hypothesis to the effect that 'all redheaded people are hypnotizable'. Scientific procedure would then require that this hypothesis be tested on a *new* group and not used to explain the data already obtained from the *original* group. For example, it is plainly circular reasoning to conclude that the individuals who had been found to be hypnotizable were so because they were redheads! Sometimes pseudo-hypotheses are formulated. These are statements that cannot be tested; that is, cannot be proved or disproved, and therefore are obviously non-scientific. As an illustration of this latter point it has been said that non-susceptible subjects are non-susceptible because of unconscious resistance, but no method of measuring unconscious resistance is indicated. In similar fashion the literature on hypnosis frequently includes

RESULTS — GROUP A

Substantiation of hypothesis from results a l r e a d y o b t a i n e d from *original* group A (circular reasoning)

HYPOTHESIS

RESULTS — GROUP B

Substantiation of hypothesis from results of *new* group (prediction)

A possible logical fallacy.

a statement that a technique is good or poor depending upon whether or not a good or poor hypnotic state has been induced. Such reasoning is after the facts (called *post hoc*), circular, and non-scientific. A similar situation is involved when we describe certain individuals, *after having first ascertained the results of susceptibility to hypnosis,* as being consciously willing but unconsciously unwilling to be hypnotized, or conversely as consciously unwilling but unconsciously willing to be hypnotized. By similar circular and non-scientific reasoning negative results are sometimes explained (away) by saying that the subject was under- or over-cooperative or had or had not an inherited tendency to susceptibility. By resorting to this kind of logic one cannot miss, and the resultant explanations represent nothing more than playing with words.

Another fallacy in logic is to assume that in a clinical case what is nearest in time to the cure has brought about the cure. For example, if therapy A has been tried and then therapies B and C attempted, all without success, and finally hypnotic therapy D does succeed, to attribute the cure to hypnotic therapy D may be an error. The cure may be due to the delayed action of A or B or C, or more probably may be due to the combination of all four therapies.

A difficulty which often arises in hypnotic work concerns the depth of hypnosis achieved. One experimenter may work with a light, a second with a deep, and a third with a very deep degree of hypnosis (ch. V). Comparison of results thus obtained may well be debated. Before results can legitimately be compared, quantification of the depth of hypnosis, by an adequate scale, must first be made. Merely describing a hypnotic state by an adjective (fairly deep, etc.) is like ordering something greenish or reddish for camouflage purposes or describing a person as having good intelligence – what is meant is never clear. It is not only important to specify the depth of the hypnotic state one is working with, but it is important to derive laws about hypnosis based on results obtained from the experiments utilizing all degrees of hypnotic depth – light, medium, and deep.

SOME POSITIVE CASES

The possibility of obtaining scientifically sound results has already been indicated. An approach which some consider unorthodox but which illustrates the application of scientific methodology to hypnosis has been reported in the European literature. A clinician was able effectively to eliminate leucorrhoea (a disturbance in females accompanied by the discharge of a certain type of mucus from the vagina) by hypnotic suggestion. The question, however, still remained as to whether or not the leucorrhoea would in time have disappeared by itself. This problem is not confined to hypnosis alone. In short, there were two factors present – the passage of time and the use of hypnotic suggestion. Which was the effective factor in eliminating the leucorrhoea? The clinician showed quite definitely that it was the hypnotic suggestion. He did this by suggesting in hypnosis that the leucorrhoea return after he had first removed it. When it reappeared, he once more made it disappear. A similar result has been reported for eczema. In this case, return of the eczema was suggested six months after it had been eliminated. Such experimental manipulations might be considered unethical by some, for once the disturbance has been removed it may be argued that it should be left that way. However, to utilize a therapeutic procedure of unknown effectiveness may also be considered unethical. It was only by the procedure described above that an answer to the question could be given.

SCIENTIFIC USES OF HYPNOSIS

SYMPTOM SELECTION

Hypnosis may also be used in an auxiliary or adjuvant sense, that is as a helper. In one case hypnosis was employed as an aid in attempting to derive an answer to a rather knotty scientific problem in psychology – the enigma of organ selection. This problem asks why it is that one person, when confronted with a conflict, breaks down in one way, say an ulcer, while another individual, confronted with what appears to be a similar conflict, breaks down in another way, say high blood pressure. There have been numerous attempts to answer this puzzling problem – body type, action of the nervous system, kind of nervous system, heredity, pseudo-heredity, as well as many other interpretations.

Hypnosis was used in the following manner in an attempt to answer this question. In hypnosis a conflict situation was suggested to the subject, and it was then observed whether there was any relation between the nature of the physiological or psychological symptoms which developed and the nature of the personality of the individual developing this symptom. While the numbers involved in this investigation were few and to a certain extent scientific rigour was lacking, it does suggest an approach, and its results are provocative. Needless to say, in such an experiment the subjects were kept under strict medical surveillance.

46

Another and still different function to which hypnosis has been put is to be seen in the experiment involving the eliciting of different moods and their effect on the individual. The subject in hypnosis is requested to tell a story to a particular picture, say of a wounded soldier being transported to a waiting aeroplane. It was found that when an optimistic mood had been suggested in hypnosis, the story usually had as its theme the advance of medicine and as its outcome the recovery of the patient. When a pessimistic mood was engendered, the story would entail as its theme the futility of war or man's inhumanity to man, and as its outcome – death. Again, however, the lack of certain controls make the results only suggestive.

The role of mood in intelligence testing may be important, but is seldom taken into consideration. One may suspect that moods (elated or depressed), or for that matter expectancy of results (high or low) or attitude to the tester (like or dislike), may affect results. Whether they do or not is not known. Hypnosis offers the possibility of controlling such variables as mood, expectancy, and attitude. Unfortunately, however, its very introduction possibly adds a new variable – hypnosis. It may be argued that even if we were replacing three variables by one, might not this new variable have a greater effect on results than the three others? Clearly investigation of this point is needed.

PERSONALITY MECHANISMS

Hypnosis has been able to provide rather unusual and highly provocative insights into certain mechanisms of personality, two of which will be described. Slips of the tongue are thought to result from only partially complete repression (thrusting out of consciousness). When this situation obtains, slips of the tongue, of which the individual may or may not be conscious, may occur. In hypnosis it was suggested to a member of an audience that he would listen to the speaker who was to address them with an increasing sense of impatience and a growing hostility. To counter this, it was suggested that he would also have a sense of respect for the speaker as well as the duty of being polite. In this situation, which attempted to duplicate the theorized conditions necessary for a slip of the tongue to occur, such a slip was obtained. The subject asked the speaker if, since he felt a draught, it would be all right for him to shut the bore (door). In addition to showing the mechanism involved in slips of the tongue, hypnosis has also been used to clarify the mechanisms underlying ambivalence – the simultaneous existence of two opposing tendencies. In hypnosis it was suggested to a smoker that he would both want to and not want to smoke at the same time. Reasons for these two attitudes were then given, and the hypnotized subject was told that after he awakened he would experience all of these feelings. Observation of the individual's waking behaviour was then made. In fairly rapid succession the subject refused an offered cigarette saying he preferred his own brand, could not find his own brand, could not find his matches, on lighting a match proceeded to get involved in a conversation and let the match burn out, on lighting the match for the second time sneezed and blew it out, incorrectly lit his cigarette which promptly went out, when the cigarette was properly lit accidentally knocked the burning tip off, and finally was observed to abandon the cigarette before it was smoked down to a reasonable butt. Unfortunately the absence of a control for the question whether this could have been done by a non-hypnotized person makes the above case only suggestive.

THE QUESTION OF SHAMMING

Probably the most frequently mentioned variable said to be introduced by hypnosis is conscious simulation. Esdaile many years ago in discussing this question in relation to surgery asks why, if it is believed that the patient is shamming (consciously simulating insensitivity), there should ever be any difference in the patient's behaviour in a first or second operation. It is especially significant if pain is shown in the second operation, for by then the patient has had the practice and knows what is expected. In a further extension of the same argument, Esdaile raised the question of how to account for the increased number of patients coming to him at the hospital. He answered this question very clearly as follows: 'I see two ways only of accounting for it; my patients on returning home either say to their friends similarly afflicted "What a soft man the doctor is! He cut me to pieces for twenty minutes and I made him believe that I did not feel it. Isn't it a capital joke? Do go and play him the same trick." Or they may say to their brother sufferers, "Look at me; I have got rid of my burden (20, 30, 40, 50, 60, or 80 lb., as it may be [scrotal tumours]), I am restored to the use of my body and can work for my bread. This, I assure you, the doctor did when I was asleep, and I knew nothing about it." ' The problem of shamming or conscious simulation is most clearly answered in this question of anaesthesia (see also chaps. I, X).

Two final notes of caution. In the enthusiasm of demonstrating that hypnosis is a bona-fide phenomenon, one should never make use of the face-backward logic which in effect says that science is often slow to accept or may reject the unusual, and therefore if hypnosis is slow to be accepted it is by this reasoning scientific. Finally, it is pompous to assume that all behaviour can be explained either by resort to interpretations at the conscious or unconscious level, and not allow for the possibility that an area of ignorance still exists.

*

The use in hypnotic induction of a standard situation – similar time periods, identical techniques, a scale of hypnotic depth, as well as an appropriate experimental design – should characterize hypnotic research. Case histories, when used, should be greater in number, and when concerned with hypnotic therapy should involve longer follow-ups. Observance of such precautions can lead only to sounder and better conclusions. As has been indicated, the scientific method of the laboratory is not always directly applicable to the problems confronting us in hypnotic research. Such qualification should mean not the absence of rigorous scientific methodology but merely the use of a different type. It is only by adherence to such scientific principles that we can be confident of any conclusion concerning the relationship between hypnosis and any other psychological variable. Inasmuch as not all the traditional scientific procedures can be utilized, data from hypnotic experiments require careful and cautious evaluation.

Finally and in summary, it may be mentioned that while data from hypnotic experiments require caution in their evaluation, the present-day emphasis on scientific procedure may also be derelict. It may well be that the *imposing of,* rather than the *describing of,* variables need not be the *sine qua non* of scientific procedure. For example, in a problem concerned with the relationship, if any, between dental cavities and certain dimensions of personality, traditional scientific procedure might imply the need for imposing cavities or anxiety. Clearly with regard to the former, this is not feasible. The problem, however, should not be ignored, but rather the relationship between these two variables should be studied. While different conclusions may be obtained by the procedures of imposition and description, they are none the less both important.

The present conception of scientific procedure requires a broader interpretation if it is to be used in the field of hypnosis.

Chapter IV

HYPNOSIS AND DEHYPNOSIS

THE purpose of this chapter is not to teach the induction of hypnosis; there are many qualified and unqualified sources that do this. Its aim is to indicate some of the facts about the nature of hypnotic induction. In order to do this it is necessary to describe the procedure for inducing hypnosis. While induction is not a difficult matter, its simplicity may be misleading. If one were asked to go for a ride in a plane and said, 'I didn't know you knew how to pilot a plane', the reply, 'Well, I know how to get it off the ground', would not be reassuring. In hypnosis the situation is similar, for what happens after hypnosis has been induced is important.

More prevalent in the past but still with us, especially in popular demonstrations, is the idea that stroking (passes) of the forehead or other parts of the body and breathing on the subject is essential for hypnotic induction. The direction of such passes was said to be important for either the onset (downward) or the termination (upward) of hypnosis. It was said at that time that by means of this physical contact 'animal magnetism' or the healing aura in clinical work flowed into the ailing person from the healthy individual. Nowadays we would in all likelihood describe such passes as producing a certain type of monotonous stimulation, in this case of the skin. Accompanying these 'passes' was much rigmarole; for example, the would-be-healer was instructed to gaze at the centre of the patient's organ of individuality, which was supposed to be situated between the eyebrows. In addition to the physical contact allowed by 'passes', animal magnetism was said to flow from one individual to the other by means of their knees which had to be touching. Techniques of induction in the older era were replete with strange ideas and procedures. Nowadays hypnotic induction relies mainly upon verbal suggestion. The technique of hypnotic induction which the writer uses is not one which he can claim as being obviously superior to any other – the existing data do not allow such a conclusion. The necessity of any particular aspect of any procedure for hypnotic induction can be debated, for there exists no systematic study of the need for different aspects of any system, and many procedures, sworn by and popular in their time, are now in disuse.

INDUCTION OF HYPNOSIS

PRESENT-DAY TECHNIQUES

Individual. First the subject, or patient as the case may be, is asked to sit down in a chair which is preferably but not necessarily comfortable. Lights are turned down and the room is relatively quiet. The subject is then asked whether he has any questions that concern him about the nature of hypnosis. If he has, these are answered briefly. Special attention is given to questions concerning the relationship between susceptibility to hypnosis and gullibility, low intelligence, or the possible dangers of repeated hypnosis. If experimental subjects are used, they are told in addition that no personal questions will be asked. If clinical subjects are used, they are told that a deep state of hypnosis in which one forgets everything that takes place is not essential for therapeutic purposes. Both clinical and experimental subjects are told that at no time will they lose consciousness, and are asked to cooperate with the experimenter. The subject or patient may also be told during induction that he will not fall asleep in the usual sense of the word, and that he will be able to talk without coming out of the hypnotic state. Again it should be emphasized that the necessity of any of the above steps or of those that follow may be debated. All that can be said is that they are utilized and that they seem to be pertinent. The actual procedure of hypnotic induction now starts:

'I want you to listen carefully to what I say, I want you to listen carefully to what I say, your eyes are closed,[1] your eyes are closed, you are feeling comfortable, relaxed, thinking of nothing, nothing but what I say, your eyes are closed, comfortably closed, you are

52

thinking of nothing, nothing but what I say, your arms and legs feel heavy,[2] your arms and legs feel heavy and you are relaxed, relaxed, your whole body feels relaxed, your whole body feels relaxed, the muscles of your face, arms, and legs are relaxed, your whole body is relaxed, it feels as though you are going backward into the darkness, backward into the darkness, and as you go backward into the darkness you are more and more relaxed, more and more comfortable, you are going backward and backward, backward and backward into the darkness and as you go backward you feel more and more comfortable, more and more relaxed, you are listening only to my voice, only to my voice, thinking of nothing, absolutely nothing, concentrating only on my voice, listening only to what I say, listening only to my voice, you are feeling comfortable and relaxed, comfortable and relaxed, comfortable and relaxed, and as you go backward and backward into the darkness you begin to feel drowsy, very drowsy, and you are thinking of nothing, nothing but the sound of my voice, you feel comfortable and relaxed, comfortable and relaxed, comfortable and relaxed, breathing regularly and deeply,[3] regularly and deeply – regularly and deeply – thinking of nothing, nothing but the sound of my voice – breathing regularly and deeply, regularly and deeply, regularly and deeply, and you are going into a sleep, a deep, sound, comfortable sleep – a deep sound comfortable sleep, breathing regularly and deeply, regularly and deeply, regularly and deeply – your sleep is getting deeper, deeper, deeper, and as you go backward into the darkness your sleep is getting deeper and deeper – deeper and deeper – deeper and deeper – and you feel comfortable and relaxed – listening only to my voice – breathing regularly and deeply, regularly and deeply – going into a deep, sound sleep – deep sound sleep, a deep, sound, sleep, and your sleep is getting deeper and deeper, deeper and deeper, deeper and deeper — you are going into a deep sound sleep — deep sound sleep — deep sound sleep — breathing regularly and deeply — regularly and deeply — regularly and deeply — and you are in a deep sound sleep — a deep sound sleep — sleep — sleep — sleep — sleep — sleep — and as I count from 1 to 10, as I count from 1 to 10, your sleep will get even deeper, even deeper, and as I count from 1 to 10 your sleep will get even deeper, even deeper — as I count from 1 to 10 your sleep will get even deeper — much deeper — much deeper. (1) deeper, deeper, deeper, and deeper; (2) — still deeper, deeper; (3) — deeper and deeper; (4) — still deeper; (5) — you're in a deep, sound sleep, a deep sound sleep.' Etc. (5 minute pause.)[4]

53

As he talks the hypnotist makes his voice become progressively lower, slower, softer, and more monotonous.

The four numerals inserted above are used to make certain points. Number 1 notes that the hypnotist *started* with the subject's eyes closed. To some people this may be surprising, for it is popularly assumed that causing the subject to close his eyes as a result of suggestion is an essential step in the inducing of hypnosis. Usually the subject starts by staring at a human eye or at a shiny object, possibly a coin, approximately a foot in front of and about eight inches above his line of sight. In this way a strain is put upon the eyes so that when the subject is told that his eyes are tired – they actually are! It was by this method that the writer had, in the past, started his own hypnotic inductions. It was given up for two reasons. The writer did not believe that any one aspect of induction was absolutely essential, and secondly, and possibly more important, the writer himself tended to look at the shiny object and become drowsy. Being somewhat susceptible to hypnosis himself, he feared the consequences might be embarrassing. Judging from hypnotic sessions before and after this change in procedure, no differences were noted, and it was not felt that starting the induction with the eyes closed had any appreciable effect on the nature of the hypnosis induced. If the eye-staring method is used, it may be advisable in some cases to tell the subject to stare into one rather than both of the eyes of the hypnotist. If he does not close his own eyes after the suggestion has been made that his eyes are tired and that he do so, then the hypnotist should gently but firmly close them for him. Number 2 is inserted by way of warning. The writer believes it wise to avoid arousing an emotional complex on the part of the experimental subject. For instance, if the subject is a girl who has fat legs and is sensitive about them, it probably would be unwise in the induction to mention that her legs feel heavy, for the subject may at this point have her train of thought (appropriate to the induction of hypnosis, it is hoped) disrupted. Number 3 denotes a factor which is mainly for the experimenter's benefit. The hypnotist by watching the response of the subject to the suggestion concerning breathing, that is whether he carries it out and to what extent,

54

obtains some idea as to whether the individual will or will not be a good subject for hypnosis. In addition to this behavioural clue, there are many other minimal clues which the hypnotist may observe, such as relaxation of facial muscles (to the point where the features are often changed), relaxed open mouth as against tensed closed lips, lack of initiative, spontaneous kicks with the feet (incomplete relaxation), frequent swallowing, and so on. An additional indication as to whether relaxation has occurred may be used. Here the hypnotist may lift a person's arm halfway up to the vertical position and then let go – if the subject is really relaxed the arm will fall down like that of a rag doll; if the subject is tense and not completely relaxed, the arm stays where it was lifted, half up and half down. These minimal clues are frequently used in clinical practice where it is thought important that the relationship between the hypnotist and the hypnotized be not disrupted by having the patient fail on one of the formal tests (to be described). Number 4 is to denote the fact that at this stage giving the subject no instructions for a time is thought to deepen the hypnotic state.

It may well be that the importance of any one aspect of the hypnotic induction procedure (conditions of quiet, light, comfort, etc.) depends upon the subject or patient. With the individual who is found to enter a deep hypnotic state at the outset, such precautions may be unimportant and vice versa.

Group. Is the procedure for induction of group hypnosis different from that for individual hypnosis? Generally what is involved in group work is nothing more than a louder voice! On one occasion a number of years ago, the writer was demonstrating certain of the phenomena of hypnosis. In the course of this he gave the subject a post-hypnotic signal (a request to carry out a given task at a given signal in the post-hypnotic state). When the signal was given, the subject and an individual who had been watching the hypnotic procedure both carried out the required action. The fact that hypnosis is not unidirectional, that it is not necessarily aimed at one person has, as will be shown, important clinical and experimental implications. Experimentally the fact that group hypnosis is feasible has saved much time in the selection of suitable subjects. The writer was accustomed to test sixteen subjects simultaneously, and to select from those on the basis of tests, which will be described, the one or two individuals who gave the greatest promise of entering a deep hypnotic state. This group procedure required the presence of two experimenters, one for inducing hypnosis and one for noting the degree to which a person is susceptible to hypnosis.

Modifications. Modifications both general and specific of the technique of hypnotic induction are many, and their use is said to ensure a greater likelihood of success. Two such general modifications are *feedback* and *fractionation*. Feedback, as its name implies, utilizes in subsequent hypnotic sessions the subjective feelings of the person undergoing hypnosis, and he appears to have many. For instance, the hypnotic subject may say that during hypnotic induction he 'experienced being warm all over', or that 'I seem to be looking at a rapidly receding square of white light', or that he was 'floating', or that he saw 'a continuous series of large hazy orange discs which started directly in front of the eyes and diminished slowly in size as they faded back into a grey field'. All such reports are thereafter incorporated into the procedure of induction on subsequent occasions. One may, however, use feedback even at the first induction by getting the individual to relate his subjective experiences just before he falls asleep at night. Fractionation involves the breaking up of the given time period used for the induction of hypnosis into parts. If a total of one hour is allotted for a given subject, fractionation would imply that the subject be hypnotized and awakened a number of times in the course of this one hour. Information gained by the feedback technique may also be used in fractionation.

Five types of specific modifications will now be described.

The *instantaneous technique,* also known as the 'carotid procedure', inhibits heart rate and interferes with circulation of blood to the brain. It works by pressure on a blood vessel near the ear. It is dangerous (ch. XI) in non-professional hands. Sad to relate, it is resorted to most often on the stage where time is of the essence and when the hypnotist has not brought his own subjects (ch. XII). It is a physiological technique which inside a minute makes the subject dazed, faint, confused, and responsive to suggestion. It raises the question as to what kind of physical state actually is present, and whether the condition produced is similar to that described for the hypnotic state. It also makes one wonder about the role of monotony in hypnotic induction. This procedure is not advised for anxious individuals because of its forceful and domineering characteristics. It is sometimes attempted when other techniques of induction have failed to produce hypnosis.

A second modification of hypnosis frequently used is to employ the verbal pattern described above, but without any mention whatsoever of sleep or any suggestion of drowsiness. This is generally referred to as *waking hypnosis*. The term 'sleep' denotes a loss of consciousness, which many individuals even though they are reassured seem reluctant to lose. When this modification is employed the word 'relaxation' replaces the word 'sleep'. The advantages of such a modification for anxious individuals are apparent.

A third though relatively rare modification has been referred to as the *confusional technique*. This is most often used with hypercritical subjects who are quick to deny that they experience any of the suggestions given to them by the hypnotist. What is done in this procedure is to have the hypnotist suggest in rapid succession that the subject's left arm is heavy, then light, then warm, then cold, and so on with his other three limbs. As a result of sheer confusion or possibly desperation, the subject, it is said, gives up, accepts the suggestions of the hypnotist, and becomes hypnotized.

The fourth modification of hypnosis concerns the manner in which hypnosis is induced. Should the technique be *domineering* or *cooperative*? The domineering technique, often referred to as 'male' or 'paternal' hypnosis, is based on fear and employs a cold tone of voice. Cooperative hypnosis, referred to as 'female' or 'maternal' hypnosis, is based on love or persuasion and utilizes a warm and friendly voice (we are not here concerned with whether the terms are properly or improperly used). The modification of the verbal procedure usually required in this technique is little more than resorting to more or less declarative sentences and a more or less positive inflexion of the voice. The method described by the writer has elements of both the male and the female hypnotic induction procedures.

The fifth and final modification is known as the *arm-levitation technique*. The emphasis in this procedure is on activity, the subject's attention is focused on his arm, and he is told that it will gradually rise and touch his face and that when it does he will at this point be in a deep sleep. This method, prevalent in clinical practice, is said to have the advantage of allowing the subject to set his own pace.

There may be modifications not in technique but in circumstances under which hypnosis is attempted. In the *disguise procedure* of inducing hypnosis, one takes a person from sleep into hypnosis, and at the termination of hypnosis returns the subject to sleep again without the subject's ever being aware of the fact that he has been hypnotized. The only changes needed in the technique of induction that has been described are the tone of voice (from very low to low), attracting the subject's attention by physical contact with the hands, and repeated statements that the subject will hear the hypnotist's voice, will not awaken, and will be able to talk. On one occasion when the writer arrived late for an appointment and found a student on whom he was doing hypnotic work asleep in his office, he tested the disguise procedure. He placed the subject in a hypnotic state, performed what was required, and then put the subject back to sleep again, without the subject's ever being aware of what had happened. The application of this technique in a hospital ward is apparent.

The *chaperone procedure* of hypnotic induction capitalizes on the fact that hypnosis is not necessarily directed at one person. The clinician may have decided that hypnotic therapy is the method of choice, but his patient may be unwilling to be hypnotized. In such a case he or she is asked to chaperone the hypnotic induction of a friend. The cooperation of the latter is first secured, and he acts much like a decoy by having the don't-want-to-be-hypnotized person actually expose himself to hypnotic induction. A case utilizing this procedure has been reported (ch. IX).

How long does one continue in the attempt to induce hypnosis? The answer to this question depends on many factors: whether the hypnosis is for clinical or experimental purposes, the particular hypnotist involved, and the type of work envisaged. In practice the writer has for experimental purposes adopted eight minutes. It may be asked why this particular time period was selected. The answer cannot be couched in learned or in wise terms. During an early experiment by the writer, one collaborator suggested six minutes, another ten minutes – a compromise of eight minutes resulted. Why it may be asked were six and ten minutes selected in the first place? These times seemed adequate on the basis of the particular experimenter's own past experience and in agreement with the time periods described in the experimental literature. It is generally considered wise to ask a person who states (boasts?) that he cannot be hypnotized how long hypnosis was attempted in his case. We find when we ask this question that some subjects have been subjected to hypnotic induction for a few minutes, some for a few hours. The relevance of such information for the person attempting to induce hypnosis is obvious. For therapeutic purposes the writer has used two one-hour sessions in which hypnotic induction was attempted. If the person requesting therapy showed susceptibility in this time period, well and good; if not, the writer turned to some other non-hypnotic therapeutic technique and the person was not considered as one in whom hypnosis could be induced *by this clinician utilizing this time period*. Again the question may be asked, what determined the time period in this case? The answer is very simple – the hypnotist's patience. In certain mental hospitals reports have been made that anywhere up to 300 hours (not consecutive) were required before the patient could be considered hypnotized. In cases where a profound degree of hypnosis is needed for the execution of complicated behaviour, eight hours of training of even initially susceptible subjects may be needed in order to obtain a satisfactory depth. Until we have more data we can only assume, with most but not all hypnotists, that the longer the induction time the more likely it is that the person will be hypnotized and the deeper will be the state achieved (the meaning of depth will be discussed in ch. V). This is not to deny, however, that on the first occasion and in a matter of seconds or minutes there are some subjects who go into a hypnotic state quickly and deeply, and that these same subjects on subsequent occasions do not appear to enter into a deeper hypnotic state.

SELECTION OF TECHNIQUE

What technique or modification thereof is best for a given individual? The answer in part depends upon the personality of the subject, and more importantly upon that of the hypnotist (patience, etc.). In short, the technique with which the hypnotist is most comfortable is the one indicated. It is entirely conceivable, for example, that a mild person might find the domineering technique of hypnotic induction distasteful or even impossible. It is also possible, however, that more than one technique may be needed for the same individual at different times. Thus, for example, when sick, Mr Smith may be susceptible to a domineering technique for inducing hypnosis, but when well may not be susceptible to this technique. This does not necessarily mean, as some of the early investigators thought, that he is no longer susceptible to hypnosis, but it does mean that he is no longer susceptible to this particular technique, and that another technique, possibly the cooperative one, is indicated.

It is also considered wise for the hypnotist to select that technique which coincides with the subject's belief, when expressed, as to how he will be hypnotized. Thus, if a given individual expects to be hypnotized by the arm-levitation method or by a recording tape, these techniques might be used. It is exactly at this point that the non-professional stage hypnotist may have an advantage over the more orthodox professional hypnotist. Suppose a subject expects to be hypnotized by some supernatural blue electric emanation from the eyes of the hypnotist. The stage hypnotist will have no hesitation or compunction in taking advantage of this belief, whereas the clinician or experimentalist is likely to try to dispel this erroneous conception. Conceivably the relative skill in hypnotic induction of the

60

stage versus the professional hypnotist may also be related to the types of personality attracted to the stage or to the professions. In addition, there is the very simple point that since stage hypnotists make their living by the practice of hypnosis, they are more likely to be concerned with it eight hours a day; whereas the clinician or experimentalist considers hypnosis as only one of a number of techniques, and consequently does not spend as much time in perfecting this skill. However, to believe that the stage showman is more adept in inducing hypnosis is one thing, to prove it is another.

*

What are often said to be different techniques are actually nothing but minor variations. Such common factors in hypnotic induction are usually: gradual restriction of word input (by the hypnotist), gradual restriction of motor output (by the subject), repetition for purposes of reinforcement, concentration, passage of time, and rapport. This word rapport refers to a close relationship between the subject or patient and the experimenter or therapist. Rapport is thought to be important, but again it is not clear just how it works or how important it is. Three steps seem always to be involved in hypnotic induction: preparation of the subject, actual induction, and subsequent deepening of the hypnotic state.

ACCESSORIES IN INDUCTION

Can mechanical gadgets such as metronomes (set at the speed of heart or respiration), clocks, recordings, tones, lights, and the like be utilized to induce hypnosis? Induction of hypnosis by such mechanical means alone is often referred to as physical, and may in part reflect a hangover from the days of Mesmer, when it was thought that inanimate material could be magnetized and that such material could in turn magnetize people. Nowadays mechanical gadgets are generally employed as aids to oral (psychological) induction. In most cases it is a matter of predominance, as both physical and psychological methods are generally present. The initial use of a gadget may be unwise in clinical practice because it may seem belittling to the patient to be hypnotized by a mechanical device. It would seem that the person-to-person relationship is important in the first hypnotic session. Related to the question of mechanical gadgets is the question whether one can be hypnotized by means of television. The answer would be yes, provided the subject was susceptible to hypnosis in the first place. Such a conclusion would also be true of radio. In these cases it is not so much a situation in which hypnosis is produced by mechanical means as one in which hypnosis is produced by a human who employs mechanical means. It was reported in the press that the British Broadcasting Company attempted to induce hypnosis by means of television – and succeeded.

HYPNOTISM BY TELEVISION

Hypnotism by television has been tried out on a closed circuit in the B.B.C. studies at Alexandra Palace with such success that it has been considered dangerous to try it over the air. The experiment was carried out on Wednesday by Mr Peter Casson. Two tests were made. In the first about a dozen B.B.C. staff volunteered to be hypnotized in the studio, and five of them went to sleep; but the most interesting point was that one person in a party watching a television screen in a darkened room across the corridor also fell under the hypnotic influence, although Mr Casson was not then addressing the viewing audience. In the second test, Mr Casson made a direct attempt to hypnotize six people watching the screen in the darkened room. Four of them went to sleep, and of these two needed waking up. Because of the success of this experiment and the consequent danger of hypnotizing viewers who might have no one at hand to wake them, it has now been decided that a hypnotic television broadcast would not be advisable.*

The same principle applies when a subject is hypnotized over the telephone and when, in experimental work, the hypnotist's words are presented by the playing of a recording (which is often done to keep his voice uniform).

Drugs as accessories, analogous to the use of mechanical devices for the induction of hypnosis, also make hypnosis more probable. Drugs alone do not produce hypnosis, but they do

* A press statement of the B.B.C. to the Press Association, London offices of Provincial Papers and Feature Editors (20 : 12 : 46).

seem to act as aids to the hypnotic state. Sometimes a 'hypnotic pill' (actually an innocuous sugar pill) is administered after the patient is first told that it is a potent drug for the induction of hypnosis. The success of this method when applied to refractory subjects is not known.

SUBSEQUENT INDUCTION

If the subject on the first occasion proves non-susceptible, then the entire induction procedure may again be required. If the subject is susceptible to a limited degree, there is evidence to suggest that about one-quarter of the time required originally will now be necessary. If, however, the subject is deeply susceptible, a post-hypnotic suggestion can be given to induce subsequent states of hypnosis, and thus the length of time required may be reduced to a matter of seconds even after the passage of years. It is customary to suggest to a subject in hypnosis that at the next session he will enter a deeper state.

Because induction of hypnosis may be slow and tedious, stage hypnotists rely on a post-hypnotic signal (chaps. V, XII) to reinstitute a hypnotic state, either in subjects they have brought along or in subjects developed in the past few days. Unfortunately the audience, unaware of this situation, receives the impression that hypnosis is quick. Consequently when induction is slow the hypnotist (usually a clinician) is considered by the layman to be inefficient.

GENERAL COMMENTS

A number of general points about hypnotic induction may now be made. No technique is purely mechanical; the expectancy of the subject to be hypnotized and his attitude to this or that mechanical gadget appear to be important. In point of fact, there are good grounds for believing that if the individual expects to be hypnotized, he may be hypnotized without a word being uttered! Techniques of hypnotic induction which combine visual, auditory, and touch elements may be more effective than techniques which employ only one of these. The stare or fascination method (visual) by which the subject stares into the eye of the hypnotist (eyes used to be thought to exude animal magnetism) may be unwise if the hypnotist is given to blinking. Furthermore, such a procedure allows for the faint possibility that the subject may hypnotize the hypnotist! The control of the hypnotized individual's behaviour may be transferred to another individual by so indicating in hypnosis. The general practice is to tell the hypnotized subject that Mr A will now take over, and that whatever he says will be effective. Another point of importance is that the known hypnotizable subject may generally be 'protected' against being hypnotized when he does not wish to be. His protection is a post-hypnotic suggestion (ch. V) to the effect that he cannot be hypnotized unless in the waking state he first signs a statement giving such permission. It is also wise to add to the post-hypnotic suggestion a phrase to the effect that the person will at no time lapse by himself into a hypnotic state. It is usually a good idea to tell the subject at the termination of hypnosis that the whole experience has been a pleasant one, that he feels well, and if the subject is a student, that he will be able to study effectively. To do so ensures a greater likelihood that the subject will return for further sessions. Hypnosis should not be thought of as eliciting only passive behaviour, for the subject often takes an active role in the proceedings (arm levitation). For purposes of reassurance, a prospective subject is often allowed to witness the hypnotizing of another person, although some hypnotists believe that this may merely serve to reinforce incorrect ideas. Other techniques, such as rapid breathing or writing a sentence as slowly as possible, are said to induce a hypnotic state, or at any rate a state very similar to hypnosis. Finally, it should be realized that a potential hypnotic subject may often object to this or that aspect of induction, such as having his eyes open or possibly having them closed, having to lie down on a couch (which signifies submission to many persons) or sit up in a chair, and so on. Consequently modifications of procedure are often necessary. One thing is apparent; the procedure for hypnotic induction should be pliable and the hypnotist flexible, but unfortunately most hypnotherapists favour and practice only one method of induction.

Finally and most regrettably the conclusion often arrived at is that so and so is a poor hypnotic subject, rather than suggesting the possibility that the technique of induction may have been inadequate. While such a conclusion tends to save face for the hypnotist by suggesting that the 'fault' lies with the subject, and while it conceivably may lead to investigation of the problem of the relation of personality traits and hypnotic induction, it does stand in the way of research on the different techniques of inducing hypnosis.

DEHYPNOSIS

Dehypnosis or termination of the hypnotic state generally proceeds as follows: 'In a minute I will awaken you – in a minute I will awaken you – when you awaken you will feel refreshed and alert, refreshed and alert – in a minute, in a minute I will awaken you and you will feel completely refreshed, completely alert – completely refreshed, completely alert, you are now beginning to awaken – you are now beginning to awaken, your sleep is getting lighter and lighter, much lighter, you are starting to awaken, your sleep is getting lighter, much lighter, and you are starting to awaken – as I count backwards from ten to one, as I count backwards from ten to one, your sleep will get lighter and lighter, lighter and lighter, and at the count of one you will be wide awake, wide awake, wide awake, ten – nine – eight – your sleep is getting lighter, much lighter, much lighter, seven – six – five – you are starting to awaken, starting to awaken, four, three, two, you are practically awake now, practically awake, one. You are now wide awake, wide awake, wide awake,' etc.

In waking hypnosis the words differ only slightly from the above. The individual is told that he will become completely normal.

Sometimes, however, difficulties arise in awakening the individual from the hypnotic state. Why the subject remains in the hypnotic state is not fully known. Some possible explanations might include: repugnance to post-hypnotic suggestions, resentment for revelations which may have been made, determination by the subject to show 'will power' by acting contrary to the given suggestion (especially if hypnosis is equated with submission), or because the subject gains relief by remaining in the hypnotized state. From what has been said it can be seen that dehypnosis is more likely to be a difficulty encountered in the clinical rather than in the experimental situation. But regardless of why a person refuses to come out of the hypnotic state, what can or should be done? Many solutions have been suggested at one time or another: instruct the subject to sleep it off, use mild pressure on the eyelids, expose the subject to a cold draught of air, clap your hands suddenly behind the subject's head, or in extreme cases, if in a medical setting, administer certain drugs. While the difficulties of terminating hypnosis should not be minimized, the problem faced by most hypnotists is getting a person into rather than out of hypnosis.

Chapter V

CHARACTERISTICS OF TESTS OF HYPNOSIS

SOME OBJECTIVE TESTS OF HYPNOTIC DEPTH

PROBLEMS IN PRE-TESTS

BEFORE describing tests of hypnosis, it is important to have some idea of just what hypnosis is, when it is present, and what it is we are measuring. The greatest disagreement between researchers lies in defining 'light hypnosis'. Some say that hypnosis is present only when there is amnesia (forgetting). Others say it is present if the subject cannot open his eyes when this has been suggested. Still others require the presence of analgesia (lack of sensitivity to pain). Given this rather confused and chaotic situation, it is not too surprising to find that deep hypnosis is often employed because of the more widespread agreement concerning its characteristics. Light hypnosis has been said to be present even though the hypnotized subject is unaware of having been hypnotized, and even when objective tests did not reveal its presence. Such a situation is somewhat analogous to the fable of the invisible clothes of the emperor – only the loyal of the realm could see them. Furthermore, the use of controls in light hypnosis does not yield clear-cut results. Obviously caution is required.

Of the various pre-tests which will predict a degree of objectively verifiable susceptibility to hypnosis, the sway test is probably the most successful. In this test the subject is told to stand with his heels touching. He is generally asked to close his eyes, and then told to imagine himself falling (direction is usually not specified). An instrument is then used to measure the amount of sway. The amount over and above the degree of sway ordinarily expected is then computed. The amount considered significant is six inches over expected sway. However, many individuals are found actually to fall when the suggestion is given. The degree of sway so measured and susceptibility to hypnosis are related. It is sometimes said that in this test you already have a hypnotized subject on your hands, and rather than dealing with a pre-test of hypnotic susceptibility you are actually dealing with a test of hypnotic depth. There are other pre-tests of hypnotic susceptibility which are less dependable though more familiar. Thus we have the hand-clasp test which observes the ease with which a person can unclasp his hands when suggestion to the contrary has been given, or the yawning test which notes the ease or difficulty as well as the time required to make a person yawn.

NATURE OF HYPNOTIC SCALES

Measuring the depth of hypnosis has never been a simple matter. In the early days, when surgery had to be performed, tests included making loud sounds, plucking hairs in the beard, squeezing the testes, and so on. Contributing to the complexity of this problem is the fact that many people think of hypnotic susceptibility as being all or none, and often fail to realize that there exist degrees of susceptibility. Furthermore, hypnosis constitutes a type of behaviour which is not well understood, and it is especially difficult to get agreement as to what behavioural phenomena are characteristic of hypnosis – especially in its lighter stages. Steps between forceful advertising, subtle persuasion, and light hypnosis are not always clear. We know that water usually becomes ice at 32° F., but we cannot say exactly when waking suggestion (no matter how defined) involves hypnosis.

Another difficulty lies in the failure to realize the fact that scales of hypnotic depth (to be described) may be of a hierarchical (ordered) nature. This would mean that if a subject passed test C, it could be assumed that he had also passed test A and test B. In similar fashion if he passed test D, it could be assumed that he had already passed tests A, B, and C. There are at present certain scales for measuring depth of hypnosis which make this kind of assumption (hierarchical) by which individuals reflect progressively increased depth of hypnosis as they pass successive tests. In these scales, the last test that an individual passes indicates his score or the depth of hypnosis obtained. There are other scales (non-hierarchical) that assume that any and all tests of hypnosis are approximately equal in value. In these scales the individual's score or the depth of hypnosis obtained is shown by the total number of tests passed. Considering our lack of knowledge, it may well be that this non-hierarchical scale which makes less assumptions is preferable. Both points of view or both scales, however, may in part be correct; that is, there may be something in both the hierarchical and in the non-hierarchical scales. Briefly there may be a cluster of tests at one level in which each test at this particular level may be of equal value; but there may be other clusters of tests at a higher level, and at this new level each test may have the same value, but all have a greater value than the tests at the first level. The value of each test will be higher if the level is higher, and lower if the level is lower. Something approaching this idea is assumed in the following description of tests.

PARALYSIS OF MINOR MUSCLES

After eight minutes for experimental work or more than eight minutes in therapeutic work, the hypnotist may wish to ascertain to what extent the subject is in a hypnotic state. The tests about to be described (as well as the minimal clues described in the previous chapter) give him some of the information he is after, and at the same time illustrate some of the phenomena that characterize the different depths of hypnosis. 'Now I want you to listen carefully to what I say, I want you to listen carefully to what I say, you are losing control of the muscles which open and close your eyes, you are losing control of the muscles which open and close your eyes, in a few minutes, in a few minutes I will let you try to open your eyes, I will let you try to open your eyes, in a few minutes, in a few minutes I will let you try to open your eyes, but the harder you try the more difficult it will be, the harder you try the more difficult it will be, and you will be completely unable to open your eyes, completely unable to open your eyes – the harder you try the more difficult it will be – the more difficult it will be – in a minute, in a minute, I will let you try to open your eyes, but you will be completely unable to, you will be completely unable to, etc. – now – try.' A full minute should be allowed for the subject to counteract, if he can, this suggestion. A number of things may occur after the challenge has been given : the subject may simply open his eyes – this is obviously a failure for this test. Or, the hypnotist may be rewarded by a gentle snore – he may literally have put his subject into a natural (not hypnotic) sleep! While this fortunately rarely occurs, it must also be considered a failure. Two other forms of behaviour constitute success. The subject may move every muscle but the right ones (known as active hypnosis) in the attempt to open his eyes, or he may make no attempt whatsoever and remain completely inert (known as passive hypnosis). Subsequent tests will reveal the difference between the latter situation and falling asleep. Regardless of which one of these four types of response is obtained, return of the ability to open and close the eyes, that is complete control over the muscles of the eyes, should be suggested. After this test the subject, regardless of whether he has passed or failed, is given a second test. The writer has had subjects who later proved to be capable of deep hypnosis open their eyes on the first test but be unable to challenge subsequent ones successfully. In group hypnosis (ch. IV) a written sign is held up asking those subjects who have succeeded in opening their eyes to close them once more and to relax.

PARALYSIS OF MAJOR MUSCLES

While the first test in our scale involved the inability to use certain small muscles, the next test involves the inability to use the larger muscle groups which are employed in rising from a chair. A procedure and 'challenge' similar to those described in the first test are employed. The subject is told that he will be unable to coordinate the muscles needed to rise from the chair in which he is now sitting. It might be mentioned that a large American radio corporation in a broadcast in 1955 made what appeared to be a bona-fide offer of $100,000 to a girl if she could rise from a chair in which she was sitting after she had been told, in hypnosis, that she would be unable to do so. She could not. After paralysis of a large muscle group has been suggested and an attempt has been made by the subject to break it, stock is taken of the subject's reactions to the first two hypnotic suggestions. If the subject has both opened his eyes and risen from the chair, it is customary (though somewhat arbitrary) to refrain from using further tests on this individual. Such subjects who have not responded to the first two suggestions are considered as non-hypnotizable with that specific technique, that time-limit, and that particular hypnotist. In group hypnosis it is customary to hold up a sign asking those subjects who have failed to pass the first two tests to sit quietly in their chairs with their eyes open. In both these tests, as well as in subsequent tests, return of the lost ability is always suggested to avoid the possibility of incurring problems (ch. XI). If the subject has passed one or both, further tests are then tried.

ANALGESIA

This test is presumed to reflect a deeper state of hypnosis than either of the first two. It involves a suggested lack of sensitivity to pain (analgesia) or generalized loss of sensitivity (anaesthesia). It is not always clear which is present. Furthermore, analgesia is often considered as the first stage of anaesthesia, or the two terms are sometimes used as synonyms. In this test, loss of sensitivity in one or both arms is suggested. For purposes of testing, a forceful jab with a needle (sterilized) or an electric shock (much stronger than can normally be borne) is given. The adjectives 'forceful' and 'much' should be emphasized, for it would be incorrect to test for the presence of analgesia, as one experimenter did, by 'beating on the thighs with a pencil'! If the analgesia is successful, the subject in hypnosis shows a reduced or complete lack of startle reaction (gasps, flinching, withdrawal, heart-rate increase, etc.) as compared with his nonhypnotized reactions. One well-known psychiatrist who was susceptible to hypnosis describes his reaction to this test in the following way: 'My friend remarked that my right hand became anaesthetic. I thought that he made a mistake, for I judged that it was too early for such suggestion. When he asserted that he pricked me with a needle I considered it as a deception made in order not to frighten me, for what I sensed was a touch with a blunt piece (I thought it was the edge of my watch). Returning to the waking state, I was very astonished realizing that I was really pricked.' It may be mentioned in passing that when this particular test is given, those few individuals who have deliberately played along in order to see what occurs in the hypnotic session will rather hurriedly decide they have played along long enough. This particular characteristic of hypnosis has, as will be described (ch. X), important therapeutic implications.

Attempts in the waking state to pretend or simulate lack of sensitivity to pain with regard to flinching, heart rate, and other physiological measurements have not been able to reach that degree of control which is possible hypnotically. Such a finding would indicate that more than voluntary inhibition of reaction is at work.

HALLUCINATIONS

This test involves the hypnotized subject's perception of objects which either have a changed physical reality or no physical reality at all (positive hallucinations), as well as failure to perceive objects which do have physical reality (negative hallucinations). These hallucinations may be in any sense modality, vision, audition, etc. The subject may be told that a lemon is a sweet orange, and he will eat it skin and all, and behave in all respects as though the lemon were a juicy, sweet, succulent orange! (It should first be determined that the subject is not one of those rare individuals who relish lemons.) Or to exemplify further the use of positive hallucinations, he may be told that hydrogen sulphide, an unpleasant-smelling gas, is actually an exotic perfume. He will then be observed to sniff it appreciatively. Or again he may be told that when he opens his eyes he will see a cat on the arm of his chair, and he will be observed to pet it. (Contrary to popular belief, a subject may open his eyes and appear in every respect to be completely awake and still be in the hypnotic state.) Finally, he may be told that he will not be able to see a certain Mr X who is actually in the room (negative hallucination). This last situation poses somewhat of a problem, because in order not to see Mr X at different places in the room he must see Mr X. It would seem that in order not to see he must first see! The subject's every act and word seem to indicate that with the consciousness he possesses he does not see Mr X. Subjective reports of individuals with such a negative hallucination indicate they experience either the presence in the room of something 'peculiar' with a 'not to be inquired into' aspect, or the existence of a white space for Mr X. This peculiarity is more interesting to the viewer than to the subject, who appears to find no incongruity in the situation. If this is strange and difficult to explain, consider the case of the previously pain-ridden patient who sometimes after brain operation (psychosurgery) will tell you smilingly that he still feels the pain but that it no longer bothers him! Pointing to another puzzling problem by no means gives an answer to the present question, nor is it the intent of the writer to distract one from this problem. It does, however, show that there are problems in other aspects of behaviour as well as in hypnosis where complete or even partial information is lacking.

An experiment involving hallucinated deafness was repeated by the writer for his own enlightenment. This experiment involved the shooting of a gun in a soundproof room, and the observing of what happened to recordings of heart and respiration in two deeply susceptible individuals. The experiment was performed in the following order under three different conditions: (a) when the subject was hypnotized and deafness had been suggested; (b) when the subject was not hypnotized and not expecting the shot; (c) when the subject was not hypnotized, but told to expect the shot. One subject gave the expected results; that is to say, no obvious reaction to the first but profound reaction to the second and third situations. (Before concluding with certainty that no reaction whatsoever had occurred in situation (a), the matter of instrumentation (ch. III) would have to be considered.) The other subject reacted to all three situations.

POST-HYPNOTIC SUGGESTION

This test must be evaluated for its effectiveness after the subject has been dehypnotized. The procedure by which it is instituted is as follows: the subject may be told in hypnosis that when he awakens he will have an irresistible urge to get a drink of water, to take off his shoe, to raise the shade, or to carry out some other type of act. The subject still in hypnosis is then told that this post-hypnotic behaviour is to be performed when the hypnotist gives the proper signal. Such a signal may be given by the hypnotist in many ways: running his hands through his hair, pulling his ear-lobe, taking a handkerchief out of his pocket, or some other such behaviour.

Post-hypnotic suggestion is simply tested by giving the post-hypnotic signal and observing whether the suggested post-hypnotic behaviour results. If the behaviour is carried out, then the subject is given credit for passing this particular test. Difficulty in evaluation sometimes arises when the subject actively modifies or only partially carries out the post-hypnotic suggestion. A sophisticated subject, one who has been hypnotized frequently, may recognize the presence of such a post-hypnotic signal by the automaticity of his behaviour in carrying out the required act. It may also happen that the subject has remembered the post-hypnotic suggestion, in which case it is still wise, foolish as it may feel, for the post-hypnotic signal to be given and the post-hypnotic behaviour to be carried out. Once the post-hypnotic suggestion has been carried out, the 'force' behind the post-hypnotic signal seems to evaporate. If a suggestion has been made but is not carried out, it may become bothersome. A subject once described the situation as similar to a forgotten word which is just on the tip of one's tongue. The compulsive force of a post-hypnotic signal even when recognized should not be minimized. The case is told of a young man who was told in hypnosis that at the count of three he would tug his ear-lobe. When awakened, he stated quite sarcastically that he wasn't even 'near' being hypnotized, and he then proceeded to describe in detail the post-hypnotic suggestion that he had been given. During this tirade by the subject, the hypnotist quietly counted to three, whereupon the subject was described as saying 'aw, shucks' and pulling his ear-lobe.

The use of a post-hypnotic signal is not only significant clinically, but is important for rehypnotizing, in that it may

74

preclude going through the entire hypnotic procedure on subsequent occasions. For by suggesting to the subject in hypnosis that on future occasions, whenever he is in a particular office seated in a particular chair, he will immediately go into a deep hypnotic state may save much time. It is generally wise to particularize the signal by which the subject re-enters the hypnotic state (in this case a particular chair in a particular office) in order to avoid the possibility of another person's inadvertently giving the required signal to the subject and having the latter respond, as has happened, by going into a deep hypnotic state. Such a situation could be embarrassing for all concerned. It may be asked exactly what is the nature of this post-hypnotic state. It is said to constitute a resurgence of a self-limited hypnosis. This may be shown by interfering with the performing of the post-hypnotic act and finding the subject in a state typical of hypnosis. It may further be asked how long a post-hypnotic suggestion is effective. The answer to this question depends on the nature of the problem for which the post-hypnotic suggestion is being given. The suggestion that a person remember non-meaningful material such as nonsense syllables (a vowel between two consonants, e.g. fam) and repeat it on receiving the proper signal has been reported as being effective some twenty years after it had first been suggested. On the other hand, it has also been reported that the suggestion that the patient remember in the non-hypnotic state a serious and traumatic memory revealed in therapy during hypnosis has often been of no avail even twenty minutes later. Effectiveness of a post-hypnotic suggestion in short depends upon many factors; whether, for example, it is being used to relieve chain smoking or casual smoking, how strong the individual's desire is to be rid of the smoking habit, the depth of hypnosis obtained, the phrasing of the instructions given, and so on. Spurious reasons (rationalizations) for post-hypnotic acts may often follow as a sequel to post-hypnotic behaviour, especially if the individual has had no memory of the suggestion's origin. This occurs in all probability because we prefer to think of our behaviour as being the result of fully conscious motives. For example, if a person is required post-hypnotically to take off his shoe, he may explain this behaviour by saying that his sock was bunched up and uncomfortable, or if required to take a drink, that he was thirsty. Such rationalizations are important in the study of personality, showing as they do the difference between real reasons and stated reasons in accounting for behaviour.

AMNESIA

The test of amnesia (inability to recall) is given as follows: 'You will forget everything that has occurred in the hypnotic state from the moment you sat down, you will forget everything that has occurred from the moment you sat down, you will remember nothing, you will remember nothing, you will forget everything, everything that has occurred from the moment you sat down, you will remember nothing – nothing – nothing, you will forget everything – everything, you will remember nothing – nothing – nothing,' etc.

In order to evaluate success or failure, the subject after awakening from the hypnotic state is asked to write down or tell everything that happened during the hypnotic session. He may remember most if not all of the tests (no amnesia), whether or not he was able successfully to challenge any of them. He may remember some but not all of the tests (partial amnesia), or he may remember nothing at all (complete amnesia). In the last case it is wise to do two things. First, probe to make sure that it is not a case in which the subject actually does remember what has happened but feels that he should not report (behaviourally the subject acts in a confused and hesitant way). Second, if the subject's amnesia remains intact under the probing, conduct another interview in twenty-four hours to allow for the possibility that amnesia may spontaneously break down during the interval. (In this extended time interval one has to be careful that the subject does not secure help from others in recalling the events that have taken place.)

If the amnesia still remains intact after all these precautions, does this indicate post-hypnotic amnesia? This may still be debated. For example, supposing one is required to learn certain material in hypnosis and then amnesia is suggested. Different criteria of the degree of remembering may be used. The subject may (1) be asked to repeat what was learned in hypnosis (recall), or (2) be shown various materials including the material learned to see if he can identify it (recognition), or (3) be required to learn the material again in the waking state, while note is made of the decrease in time and in errors (savings) now found. There is also evidence that the action of the nervous system (as shown by changes in heart rate, respiration, and blood pressure recorded on a machine) may reveal the presence of learning which cannot be verbalized. These criteria may indicate different degrees of learning. Sometimes either of the first two criteria (recall or recognition) may fail to reveal the presence of learning, that is show amnesia, whereas either of the latter two (savings or action of nervous system) may show the presence of learning, that is fail to show amnesia. Certainly the use of recall is more likely to reveal the presence of amnesia than the use of savings. Or conversely it may be said that savings is more likely to reveal the presence of learning than recall. Which criterion, then, should be used to indicate the presence or absence of amnesia? In practice in hypnotic work, amnesia is usually tested for its presence or absence only by the first criterion (recall), and this, as has been indicated, is the criterion most likely of the four criteria to show the presence of amnesia. Spontaneous amnesia – that is, amnesia which is not suggested and which appears of its own accord or possibly by self-suggestion and which is subject to the same criticism as induced amnesia – may also occur. Spontaneous amnesia more frequently appears in clinical cases, and is thought possibly to protect the patient from unpleasant recollections.

It is believed by some that the presence of amnesia after hypnosis is not as often a result of inherent spontaneity as it is a function of indirect (though not necessarily witting) suggestion by the experimenter or therapist.

SOME GENERAL COMMENTS

A number of points may now be made about the above tests and the different degrees of depth of hypnosis that are obtainable. Two of these points have already been stated but merit repetition. The tests are not necessarily arranged in a hierarchy; that is, they are not in a perfect ascending or descending order. Consequently the first point that should be made is that if one test has been failed further tests should still be attempted. Secondly, the hypnotist should suggest a return of the ability or sensitivity that has been made to disappear *regardless of the outcome of hypnotic induction*. Thirdly, it is generally considered wise to keep the subject in one's office for fifteen or twenty minutes after the termination of hypnosis to make certain that he is wide awake and will not injure himself by colliding with the door or some other obstacle. A test, usually employed on the stage, involves the production of muscular rigidity (catalepsy). This is produced in sufficient degree for the hypnotized subject to be laid out between two chairs, heels on one and neck on the other, and then to support a man's weight on his stomach. In the old days a mounted horse would tread on him. In either case there is danger of torn or injured muscle, and woe betide the person who is not completely rigid. In therapeutic situations, tests which might disrupt the interview are seldom if ever used. Quite recently the suggestion has been made that if you want to find out the depth of hypnosis of a given hypnotic subject – ask him while he is hypnotized! Unfortunately this simple and direct method has no proof.

What percentage can be expected to pass various tests and reach different stages denoting different degrees of depth of hypnosis? Figures given by many workers are difficult to compare inasmuch as different techniques, different lengths of time, and different hypnotists have been involved. Furthermore, as has already been pointed out, there is lack of agreement among hypnotists concerning the phenomena which are indicative of hypnosis at the lighter end of the scale of depth. Consequently the same phenomena may be said by some to indicate light hypnosis and by others not to involve hypnosis in any way whatsoever. Roughly, however, it may be said, considering limitations, and evaluating results of thousands of reported cases, that about 5 to 20 per cent of hypnotic subjects reach the deepest depth (somnambulism) and that another 5 to 20 per cent are not at all susceptible to hypnosis. The remaining 60 to 90 per cent are said to be capable of entering light or medium hypnosis.

Such figures are only approximate and are found with adults. Children (seven to fourteen years of age) are said to be more hypnotizable and consequently, if this finding is correct, figures on susceptibility would have to be revised for children. Ideally, data on susceptibility to hypnosis should be reported in terms of at least such factors as age, sex, technique of induction, time per session, number of sessions used, and so on; unfortunately they seldom are. In experimental work in order to avoid this lack of precision about susceptibility, study is often limited, as has been indicated, to those subjects who go into a deep hypnotic state (somnambules). As a result of such a situation, experimentation is lopsided and conclusions reached come predominantly from one end (deep) of the scale of hypnotic depth. Hypnotic therapy, it is true, does not require a deep hypnotic state. This, however, is a mixed blessing. It is fortunate because of the limited number capable of achieving a deep hypnotic state, but the very fact that the subject cannot achieve such a state rules out the possibility of using certain techniques. For example, a case was cited in which a homosexual incident was related in a deep hypnotic state accompanied by much emotional disturbance. The therapist did not believe that the subject's strength of personality at the time was such that he would be able to tolerate this information in the waking state. Consequently, the clinician suggested amnesia for the whole incident – a procedure which probably could not be used unless the subject could enter a fairly deep hypnotic state in the first place. In similar fashion certain other phenomena of hypnotic analysis (to be discussed later) can only be employed with subjects who enter into a deep hypnotic state.

It may also be mentioned that the figures given for the percentage of the population which enter into different depths of hypnosis indicate the impossibility of the Indian rope trick (assuming it exists) being, as it is sometimes said, a function of mass hypnosis. In this deception a person climbs a rope which stretches upwards into the air seemingly without support. In order for this to be a reflection of the use of hypnosis, all subjects in the audience would have to be capable of experiencing hallucinations – a highly improbable situation.

Finally because of the fact that we know so little about the nature of hypnosis, fine divisions of hypnotic depth are hardly justified. Tests may be thought of as reflecting at most four different stages or degrees of depth: (1) non-susceptibility, no indication of any reaction to suggestion; (2) light hypnosis, reflected possibly by eye closure, relaxation, drowsiness, regular breathing, and limb paralysis; (3) medium hypnosis, which in addition to the items already listed may be reflected by partial amnesia, partial analgesia, positive hallucinations, and the execution of simple post-hypnotic suggestions; and finally (4) deep hypnosis, sometimes referred to as somnambulism, which in addition to the above items may be reflected by the ability to open one's eyes and walk and talk, complete amnesia, complete anaesthesia, negative hallucinations, and execution of complicated post-hypnotic suggestions.

SOME SUBJECTIVE REACTIONS TO OBJECTIVE TESTS

Thus far only objective reactions to tests of hypnotic depth, those observable by more than one person, have been reported. How, it may be asked, does the subject feel? Subjects susceptible to different depths of hypnosis were asked to write descriptions of their subjective experiences. Some of the reports were taken immediately after hypnosis, some twenty-four hours later. These subjective reactions are roughly indicative of increasing depth of hypnosis. The subjects had all the tests described above, and the reports are given below verbatim. Comments in parentheses are my own.

'I sat down in the chair, was told that I was to forget everything – relax, and go into a deep sleep – think of nothing but the operator's voice. I found that I became sleepy, I was then told I was bound to my chair (paralysis of large muscles) and then told to rise. I found this very difficult, but I believe I did so – I was told I had no sensation in my right arm (analgesia). I felt a definite painful sensation. I was told to remove my shoe at the stimulus of a cough by the operator (a post-hypnotic suggestion). I was then told to come out of the sleep.'

'He told me to fall asleep, I felt pasted to the chair, I felt cold and my limbs felt numb, he told me to do things, I had the feeling I could have done them if I had only tried hard enough. Things like opening my eyes (paralysis of small muscles). He talked to me and said that I would be asked the time and that I would say it's either an hour earlier or an hour later than it actually was. I don't remember which (a post-hypnotic suggestion), but I told him the correct time.'

'I was to see a cute, friendly little kitten sitting on the arm of my chair, to pet it, and to put it on the floor (positive hallucination). On instructions to open my eyes, I did so only to find no kitten.'

'I find it extremely uncomfortable and irritating to try to remember hypnotic events.'

'My right arm felt numb, when he wrote 2 on the board I was to feel a draught, which I did (positive hallucination). I felt a slight shock on my right arm. I couldn't open my eyes, I couldn't stand, I just felt tired. It seems that I remember just about everything, the eye opening which I actually couldn't do, the body raising which I couldn't do and the rest I could do, and was aware of everything else.'

'When he asked me if I remembered anything of the trance I re- mained silent. I knew well everything what had occurred and yet when I tried to speak nothing came out. A few moments afterwards I was able to relate the whole of the experiment (probing had occurred). He challenged me to raise my arm. Needless to say, this time I really tried but succeeded only in a mass movement of my shoulder muscles and movements of my fingers all to no avail. I realize now that this was not my own desire to please the experi- menter or the class, but a complete inability to coordinate the muscles of that arm.'

'All I remember is that I felt something stinging my right arm for a fraction of a second. I don't remember anything else except a sleepy feeling and a ringing in my ears. I remember getting very relaxed. Things aren't too clear at all after that. I do remember standing up, I think. Something about my arm I remember also, but I am not sure what. I felt comfortable and peaceful, at rest. I remember chimes ringing (positive hallucination), I remember a loud buzzing, but that is all.'

'When the lights were turned on I had the queerest desire to have the shades pulled up (a post-hypnotic suggestion). I must admit I felt rather silly asking that they be pulled up, but I just knew that before I went home I would see to it that they were.'

'I felt rather anxious and apprehensive, although I was eager to go into the trance and cooperate to the fullest extent. I believed that my excitement would hinder the results, and so I intended to just play along and see what happened. I didn't try too hard to open my eyes and move my immobile right arm. However, when I tried to get up from my chair and found that I was totally unable to I was very surprised. From that time on the trance became very real. The hallucination of a book lying on the arm of the chair was very real, and I can still remember size, colour, and position of it. The burning sensation on my right arm was extremely excruciating (positive hallucination).'

'In my own case it wasn't until after I had my drink and returned to the class that I realized that it was a post-hypnotic suggestion, and even then I didn't know what I had responded to, I was simply very thirsty and had to have a drink.'

'Nothing except that I think I woke up once (not observably so).'

'Nothing.' (Complete amnesia as tested by recall.)

'I closed my eyes and tried to relax. I had just about decided that I couldn't do it and I didn't want to anyhow. Then I began to feel awfully drowsy and my eyes couldn't stay open and my arms and legs felt so very heavy, and that's about the last I know until he awoke us. A couple of minutes later (actually two hours) I was suddenly very thirsty (a post-hypnotic suggestion). I simply had to have a drink.'

Chapter VI
HYPNOSIS AND PERSONALITY

CHARACTERISTICS OF SUSCEPTIBLE AND NON-SUSCEPTIBLE SUBJECTS

ARE there any ways in which tests or pre-tests or hypnotic susceptibility may be avoided? In effect, is there any way in which we can say, by observation of individuals, that A will make a good subject and will be susceptible to hypnosis, whereas B will not be susceptible and therefore a waste of time. Are there any specific personality aspects of the individual which indicate susceptibility? There are certain characteristics of the individual which indicate some relationship with susceptibility to hypnosis, although practical considerations frequently make it simpler to attempt actual hypnosis (especially group hypnosis) in determining who is and who is not susceptible. Although the results of these (completely non-hypnotic) tests may be of questionable value from a practical point of view, they are of value theoretically, for they say something about the characteristics of susceptible and non-susceptible individuals, and thus about the nature of hypnosis.

Concerning this question of determining by non-hypnotic means just who is and who is not susceptible to hypnosis, there exist many ideas – some held by the layman, some by the professional. Many such beliefs are fictitious. It is said that if one has low intelligence or is stupid, is suggestible or is submissive, has a small degree of will power, has poor emotional stability, or possesses a low forehead – then he will be susceptible to hypnosis. While such beliefs may be widely held, few are true. The meaninglessness and the vague generalizations inherent in such beliefs are well illustrated by a magazine article in which it is stated that the most susceptible subjects are those who are either male or female! Let us examine some of these beliefs.

INTELLIGENCE

With regard to intelligence the relationship found is, if anything, contrary to that popularly expected. It would seem that of two groups of hypnotic volunteers, the group having the higher average intelligence tends, though only slightly, to have the greater number of hypnotically susceptible individuals. This finding, however, is based on college students and dental patients, a select sample from the higher socio-economic group (p. 146), and it is doubtful whether we can generalize. It may be safest to conclude that there has been no indication that the lower the intelligence the greater the susceptibility.

SUGGESTIBILITY

A moment's reflection about the use of this term makes one pause. When is a man suggestible? Is he suggestible if he wears a tie or is this merely custom? Is he suggestible when duped by a salesman or is this merely what we call submission? Is he suggestible if during an experiment he detects an odour which actually is not present, or is this merely confidence in the experimenter? Is he suggestible if in the midst of studying he accepts a friend's invitation and goes to a movie or is it merely that he is bored? Is he suggestible when he attributes a liberal statement to a labour leader rather than to a conservative individual who has actually made the statement, or is this merely the operation of intelligence? Is he equally suggestible in all areas such as business, health, sex? Is he suggestible if in word association (giving an immediate verbal response to another word) he replies with a word that is found to be frequent in the general population? Is he suggestible if he yawns when another does or when a yawn is vividly described? All the foregoing, as well as other instances, have been claimed at one time or another to be examples of suggestibility. Consideration shows that popularly and often professionally the many different psychological processes involved in the term suggestibility are often confused, and the word 'suggestion' is frequently nothing more than a wastepaper-basket for vague and ambiguous concepts.

Suggestion and its problems were the subject of a typical

chapter in the older textbooks on psychology. The omission of this topic from current texts is not a sign that the problems have been solved but that they were and still are embarrassing. Difficulty in defining the term is probably due to the fact that there are many types of suggestion. As an example of the large number of terms describing suggestion, consider the following: direct *v.* indirect, negative *v.* positive, true *v.* untrue, overt *v.* covert, prestige *v.* nonprestige, verbal *v.* nonverbal, primary, secondary, and tertiary. Some of these will be dealt with more fully in later sections of this chapter. Despite this multiplicity of types, there have been numerous attempts by many people at different times to define suggestion. It has been said that suggestion implies resistance, represents the influence of one person upon another without the latter's consent, reflects the role of impulse rather than of will, is present to a certain degree in everybody, reflects the implanting of an idea, illustrates the submissive instinct, appeals to the unconscious, is indistinguishable from education, etc. The definitions which have been proferred are varied, confusing, incomplete, and seem to reflect the old saying that to define is to limit. The complexity of the problem is further reflected by the fact that our culture plays a significant role in determining the individual's acceptance or rejection of suggestions. Thus, for example, if I were to attempt to modify the attitude that many people have towards homosexuality, I would immediately encounter the cultural suggestion (at least in some countries) that homosexuality represents a 'crime against nature' and is a perversion. Since there are many types of suggestion, it would be simpler to define each by what it stands for and by what it does.

It is also popularly thought that a hypnotically susceptible person must be suggestible in the sense of being gullible or easily taken in (in the waking state). Such a statement is ambiguous unless one specifies what kind of suggestion is meant. If this is done it is often found that the type of suggestion referred to has nothing whatsoever to do with gullibility. Popular opinion tends to think of suggestion as characterized by deceit and lying and the recipient as being a victim who has been taken in. In actual fact the type of suggestion (direct) found in hypnosis has no relation to the type of suggestion (indirect) which possesses these attributes. Hypnosis depends upon an entirely different type of suggestion, one which is straightforward and obvious. It can even be questioned whether the term suggestion should be used at all with regard to hypnosis, inasmuch as the type of suggestion involved is so much different from what is popularly assumed to be suggestion. This confusion or ignorance probably accounts in part for the debatable status of hypnosis in professional circles today; the repeatedly encountered boast 'I'll bet you can't hypnotize me', made by the person who glories in his so-called 'will power' and in his ability to resist being 'taken in'; and the suspicion and scorn with which highly hypnotizable subjects are regarded.

Scientists working with groups of patients have by mathematical means, which need not concern us in this book, separated out at least two and possibly more types of suggestion. The first type of suggestion that they found corresponds to direct suggestion and shows a positive relationship with hypnosis. In short, it can predict susceptibility. This type of suggestion, not commonly thought of as suggestion, is illustrated by the body-sway test (p. 67). The second type of suggestion found is the indirect type and corresponds to what is usually thought of as suggestion. It shows no relationship whatsoever to hypnosis. This form of suggestion is illustrated by the odour test. In this test deception and misleading cues are used, and the subject is led to report smelling a substance that just is not there. For example, an instructor may walk into the classroom, announce that today he wishes to demonstrate the speed with which an odour is diffused throughout a room, proceed to uncork odourless coloured water and ask students to raise their hands when they detect an odour. In this type of indirect suggestion, if one has seen it done to another person, read about it, or been told about it, the effect is destroyed. In the direct suggestion of hypnosis, on the other hand, all these things (watching, reading, or being told) may occur without destroying the effect. For example, it is often of value to have the subject actually see another person being hypnotized.

Some hypnotists, in their desire to differentiate between these two forms of suggestion and to prohibit any aspect of indirect suggestion being involved in hypnosis have advised other hypnotists to preface all challenges or tests by the words 'as if'. Thus, in the first test one might say that the eyes cannot be opened because it is *as if* they were glued down. In this way they believe that even the slightest appearance of deception, associated with indirect suggestion, can be avoided. It can be debated whether this terminological difference really makes a difference.

In the induction of hypnosis, elements of indirect suggestion may actually be present in other than the verbal pattern. It is customary in inducing hypnosis to tell the subject, who may be fixating an object some eight to twelve inches away and above the line of sight, that his eyes are tired and they will close – they usually are and do because of physiological rather than psychological reasons. Or, again, consider the hand-clasp test where the fingers of one hand are interlaced with those of the other. The statement is made that one cannot unclasp one's hands. Inability to do this has a physical explanation – the knuckles are larger than the bones of the fingers and make unclasping somewhat difficult. Other techniques involving the use of indirect suggestion are sometimes used to 'impress' the naïve individual and to increase his confidence in the hypnotist and so make him more susceptible. In all probability both physiological and psychological factors are at work in the individual's reactions.

SUBMISSIVENESS

It is also assumed by many that to be a hypnotically good subject is to be submissive. This belief probably stems from the previous idea that to be hypnotically susceptible you must be gullible (indirect suggestion), and probably adds the statement that to be gullible is to be submissive. Inasmuch as susceptibility to hypnosis is unrelated to indirect suggestion, it would be surprising if hypnosis and submission were actually related. Such a relationship was only assumed to be present because of the confusion that exists between hypnosis and indirect suggestion. The problem was, nevertheless, investigated, and tests of submission given to subjects who had been shown to be susceptible to hypnosis. The results showed no relation whatsoever between hypnotic susceptibility and submissiveness.

TRIADIC HYPOTHESIS

This theory holds that three personality factors go together more often than would be expected by chance. These factors are: susceptibility to hypnosis, impunitiveness (avoiding aggressive behaviour), and repression (excluding unacceptable ideas from consciousness). Individuals susceptible to hypnosis have been found to be impunitive; that is, in a situation involving conflict they blame neither themselves (intropunitive) nor others (extrapunitive), but find a logical reason for the occurrence of the particular act. They also use repression as a favourite method of defence when confronted with conflict. The theory holds that for too long we have sought for variations in susceptibility to hypnosis to be related to *one* personality factor, while all along we should have been looking for variations in susceptibility to be related to *many* personality factors.

How exactly, it may be asked, is the direction of punitiveness indicated or how is repression measured? An example from the former will indicate how this particular test is scored. A cartoon picture of a man walking on the pavement and being splashed by a passing car is shown. Above the man's head is an unoccupied 'balloon' which is to be filled in by the subject, who in so doing gives the man's (essentially his own) reaction to the situation. If the subject writes down that the man has said to the occupants of the car, 'Why don't you watch where you're going?', this is extrapunitive, for it directs the blame to the outside. If, on the other hand, the subject indicates the man to be saying that this will in effect teach him not to walk near the kerb, such an answer is in the direction of being intropunitive. If, however, the subject indicates, in this empty balloon, that the driver had to do this to avoid running over a dog, this would be impunitive, for it neither blames the driver nor himself, but finds a legitimate reason for the occurrence of the splashing. Repression is measured by seeing which of twelve puzzles the subject remembers. He purposely (but this was not known to him) was made to succeed in six and fail in six. Predominance of remembering successful rather than failed puzzles is characteristic of repression.

OTHER PERSONALITY FACTORS

With regard to will, little can be said since the very concept itself is not clear or meaningful. In connexion with emotional stability, there is no evidence that emotional stability or instability makes one more or less susceptible to hypnosis. The idea that having a low forehead makes one more susceptible to hypnosis can only be said to be a remnant of the old-time physiognomy when it was said that a person's character could be read from the bumps on his head or by the gross shape of his body. Data concerning the influence of sex, age, and mental disease on the question of susceptibility to hypnosis are conflicting and unsatisfactory. In general, there appears to be a slightly greater tendency for women to be more susceptible than men. Such a finding, however, may be spurious (see later section in this chapter). Eight years of age is said to be the most susceptible stage in life, and over fifty the least. An individual who is susceptible to hypnosis tends to give or project stories to stimulus cards with hypnosis as a theme and with the outcome of the hypnotic induction being successful. Confronted with a similar situation, the non-susceptible individual will either tend to give a story unrelated to the theme of hypnosis or, if hypnosis is involved, there will be a negative outcome for the attempted induction. Purported differences in susceptibility as related to nationality have never been satisfactorily shown. It is frequently said that sleep-walkers or sleep-talkers or possibly ouija-(witch-) board performers are susceptible to hypnosis. What little evidence there is does not support this notion. Other normal personality variables share this rather nebulous situation.

There is no good evidence that the psychotic is more or less susceptible to hypnosis than the mentally healthy person. In point of fact, a strait-jacket or some kind of restraint has some-times been used on non-manageable psychotics to induce fatigue, whereupon hypnosis was achieved successfully. While there is at present a fair amount of agreement that psychotics can be hypnotized, the depth which they can reach is disputed. Some die-hards who maintain that psychotics cannot be hypnotized will, if they are successful in hypnotizing a psychotic, change their diagnosis of the individual from psychotic to neurotic! It is often stated that the mentally deficient or the feeble-minded cannot be hypnotized, but such a conclusion is reached in the absence rather than the presence of data.

THE NON-SUSCEPTIBLE

Are there any definitive factors which indicate a lack of susceptibility? If there are, they again are not clear. Before failure in induction can be considered final there must be consideration of adequate time (in one case 300 hours was required), variety of hypnotic induction techniques used (different techniques may be required according to whether the subject is sick or well), and different hypnotists (an individual may be susceptible to hypnotist A but not to B). When such factors are taken into consideration, it is not too surprising to find reports of success in the hypnotic induction of alcoholics, seniles, syphilitics, and psychotics of various kinds.

Even when all these precautions have been taken, there may still be resistance to hypnotic induction. Subjects may resist for various reasons: the procedure may elicit an emotional complex; hypnosis may be associated with letting go sexually; there may be fear of possible revelations; there may be unrecognized antagonism; or there may be reasons unknown to both subject and experimenter, patient and clinician. Such resistance may be shown by shivering, restlessness, actual sleep, coughing, or verbal depreciation of the effectiveness of hypnosis. If more were known about the various reasons for resisting hypnosis, we should at the same time know more about hypnosis. Partial resistance may show itself by a difficulty in dehypnotizing (p. 65) or by lighter depths of hypnosis.

HYPNOTIZABILITY OF HYPNOTISTS

Some fifty of the 'leading authorities' in the field of hypnosis were polled in an attempt to find out whether they considered themselves good hypnotic subjects. The belief prevails that hypnotists themselves make poor subjects, and although the poll lacked a definition of hypnotic depth, results were in the direction of supporting this belief. The reasons advanced by these fifty hypnotists varied: some said there had been no attempt to hypnotize them, some stated that they were too analytical and tended to evaluate the procedure being tried, and a small number feared the unknown! Of course, one could always question whether the really real reasons were given!

Summarizing this and other data on what may well be a select sample, we can say that the hypnotically susceptible individual is neither gullible nor submissive, possesses a slightly higher intelligence relative to the non-susceptible subject, is motivated to see successful hypnosis in picture cards, tends to be impunitive, and to use repression as a means of personality defence. There is the very definite possibility that we might have to modify our conclusions for different degrees of susceptibility. In saying this about the individual, we have at the same time said something about the nature of hypnosis itself. It is in this fashion, it is hoped, that the nature of hypnosis will be more fully comprehended in the future.

CHARACTERISTICS OF VOLUNTEERS AND NON-VOLUNTEERS

Interestingly enough, volunteers for hypnosis (individuals who have not been exposed to susceptibility tests) share similar personality traits with actually known hypnotically susceptible subjects. Such traits differentiate volunteers from non-volunteers in the same way that susceptible and non-susceptible individuals are distinguished. In one empirical study it was found that volunteers for hypnosis possessed higher intelligence, had less anxiety, were more (not less) dominant, and were less prejudiced in general than non-volunteers. Equally important was the finding that in introversion-extroversion and sociability differences were not found.

*

Results which have been referred to in this chapter (characteristics of susceptible subjects and volunteers for hypnosis) would certainly argue against the popular picture of the hypnotic subject as a submissive inferior person. If anything, the data would suggest, at least in experimental subjects, that hypnotic individuals are better adjusted than those who refuse to be hypnotic subjects.

The pendulum thus has swung (or should swing) from the popular image of the hypnotizable person as inferior to the position that he is superior. At the very least it could be argued that the personality tests currently available indicate a lack of differences between hypnotic and non-hypnotic subjects.

CHARACTERISTICS OF THE HYPNOTIST

Is there anything about the experimenter or therapist that makes one a good hypnotist, another a poor hypnotist? Again there exist many fictitious beliefs. A good hypnotist, it is said, will have some if not all of the following characteristics: he will be tall, he will be dark-complexioned, he will have black foreboding eyes, he may be slightly mad, he will be a foreigner (in whatever country he is in!), he should suffer neither from 'youthful immaturity' nor 'senile decrepitude', but should be 'broad of shoulder' and show 'superior muscle development'! He also would be well advised to possess 'benevolence' so that he will undertake all types of cases, 'conscientiousness' so that his motives may be of the purest type, 'firmness' to meet difficulties, 'caution' to plan prudently, and 'lofty veneration' to achieve ultimate success. To be a hypnotist one should, according to this last recipe, be a paragon of virtue and perfection.

Such descriptions are completely irrelevant and without foundation in fact. The need for the hypnotist to possess the ability to concentrate if he is to produce hypnosis is again a misconception. The hypnotist may, in fact, be thinking of last night's poker game while he is inducing hypnosis. Are there any characteristics, then, which hypnotists should possess? In the opinion of the writer the hypnotist needs first of all, and this is true of any professional field, knowledge of the subject-matter so that he is aware among other things of the different types of induction and when to use them. Second, he should have had actual experience with hypnotic induction in order to evaluate and meet different situations. Third, he should be fairly well adjusted so that there will be no danger of a Messiah complex (being over-impressed by his own ability or power). Being aware of his own personality characteristics, he is more likely to understand which hypnotic technique best suits his own personality. Finally, and probably most important, he should possess a great deal of patience, so that he will devote as much time as is necessary for hypnotic induction.

CHARACTERISTICS OF THE RELATIONSHIP BETWEEN SUBJECT AND HYPNOTIST

We have looked at some of the characteristics possessed by the subject and a few of the characteristics needed by the hypnotist – attributes which are assumed to be possessed *independently* of each other. What, then, of the attributes each possesses which more obviously *depend* upon the other, and which no amount of analysis of the hypnotist alone or of the subject alone would reveal? Admittedly such analysis is difficult, but data of this kind may well supplement (not supplant) our information received from consideration of the more obvious independent factors. Deciding what is an independent or dependent factor is not always easy – especially since a given characteristic may have elements of both. Generally it is a question of predominance. Age might be an example of an independent factor. Sex would be an example of a factor which has to be evaluated as to what attributes belong to the dependent and what attributes belong to the independent category. Certainly one is a male or a female regardless of the sex of the hypnotist. It is in this sense that sex, like age, may be considered as an independent factor. However, the manifestations of sex, especially in our culture, may be contingent upon the sex of the hypnotist, and therefore certain aspects of sex would have to be considered as dependent factors. Feelings of anxiety engendered by the hypnotist would exemplify the dependent factor.

Previously it was stated that the available data indicates that there might possibly be a slight sex difference, the female being more susceptible to hypnosis than the male. It is also possible, however, that this may be a spurious finding. The conclusion that there is a sex difference in hypnotic susceptibility is reached on the basis of analysis of data from independent characteristics. Supposing the data were to be analysed also on the basis of dependent characteristics, what then? If one were to do this, then one would ask whether a female hypnotized by a male (different sex) or by another female (same sex), or a male hypnotized by a male (same sex) or by a female (different sex), would be more or less susceptible. In short, one would be asking whether being hypnotized by a person of the same or of different sex would yield different results. Analysis would now be based on dependent characteristics as well. The relationship that is customarily reported wherein the female is said to be more susceptible to hypnosis than the male might be revealed as spurious by such an analysis of dependent factors, for most of the hypnotists today are males (of eighteen men and eighteen women, asked to draw a hypnotist, only one drew a woman). Independent analysis ignores this fact, and merely asks what percentage of males and what percentage of females is susceptible to hypnosis. It is conceivable that if the majority of hypnotists were female, the males might then be found to be the more susceptible of the two sexes if analysis of independent factors only were made.

What effect on susceptibility to hypnosis does the personality of the hypnotist have on the subject and vice versa? At present we are quite sure that the personality of the hypnotist, like his sex, has an effect not only on the depth of hypnosis but also on the question of susceptibility itself. In short, X may enter a deep hypnotic state with hypnotist A, a light one with B, and fail completely to enter a hypnotic state with hypnotist C. Unfortunately, the data we have bearing on the question are arrived at after the results are known and not by prediction. We are not only unable to evaluate the effect of one type of personality on another and what effect it has on hypnosis (dependence analysis), but we even encounter difficulty in obtaining agreement as to what exactly constitutes personality. The problem of whether or not successful induction needs the presence of prestige (a personality characteristic) in the relationship between subject and experimenter has been raised. To those that say that prestige is a necessary element in the hypnotic relationship, it should be pointed out that most hypnotists who possess prestige also possess good technique. Consequently, two factors are present, technique as well as prestige, and it would be gratuitous (as well as poor scientific logic) to point to only one. Results do not indicate that the presence of prestige is essential. In addition, the very fact that one can predict susceptibility to hypnosis from situations clearly not hypnotic in nature, and that different hypnotists can obtain roughly the same depth, indicates that hypnosis is a function of the individual as well as of the hypnotist. The hypnotist may be *a* but is certainly not *the* factor in hypnosis. The last two points indicate that independent factors as well as dependent factors are important in determining susceptibility.

Granted such limitations, for obviously not all relationships suggested by analysis of dependent factors will be significant, it still would be profitable to have future research take into account the relationship between the hypnotist and the subject which is dependent in nature. In this way additional information could be added to the data derived by analysis of independent factors in the quest for knowledge about the nature of hypnosis.

Chapter VII

THE GENERATION OF HYPERS

THIS chapter asks whether greater than usual (hyper) ability can be generated in hypnosis, and if so, what its nature is. There is also the question whether this supranormal ability, if it exists, appears as a result of hypnosis alone or whether its appearance requires suggestion in hypnosis. Findings in this area by early researchers were quite positive. However, more recent experiments, with better controls, are not quite so positive. Furthermore, recent work gives a different interpretation of the results. Science at present requires that every new degree of ability, whether muscular or sensory, be distinct from that found in the individual's everyday behaviour. In this insistence by science, as will be shown, lies the key to the difference in interpretation.

INCREASED MUSCULAR POWER
(HYPERBRAXIA)

The question here is whether or not strength, in the form of muscular ability, is increased by the use of hypnosis. Fabulous feats of strength are supposedly performed by hypnotized individuals. One hears of the subject who, when rigid (cataleptic) and placed across two chairs, supports a heavy weight in the abdominal region. It is important to realize, however, that catalepsy can be induced in the waking as well as in the hypnotic state. Cases in which increased muscular hand strength are reported are numerous. While many of these reports are probably genuine, they fail to take into account the difference that exists between actual output (performance) and potential output (capacity). Thus, for example, in muscular strength of hand grip the actual output may be only sixty pounds pressure, whereas we would assume that potential output would be greater, possibly in the neighbourhood of seventy pounds pressure. Most actual output in the waking state is below potential output, and hypnosis may be favourable to performance approximating the individual's capacity. In short, it is suggested, on the basis of observations of behaviour under stress, that individuals are capable of more than they normally show, and that this increased muscular ability might appear not only in hypnosis but in the waking state as well, provided the individual was sufficiently motivated. A good example of this problem is the aerial acrobat who is able to perform many amazing feats with his jaw muscles. In this characteristic, the acrobat's actual output approximates his potential output, whereas in most of us our actual output is far below our potential output, at least as far as the jaw muscles are concerned, and generally in most other motor and sensory abilities. Sometimes what appears to be an increase in muscular power is not so much an increase in muscular power as it is the absence of pain or feelings of fatigue which permit of the appearance at least of improved performance. How long one can maintain his arm outstretched in a horizontal position exemplifies this problem. Hypnotized subjects, while not able to do this any longer (six minutes) than non-hypnotized subjects, behaved differently in the amount of tremor observed. The hypnotized subjects showed less tremor of the arm and did not report the presence of pain.

The possibility of differentiating actual behaviour in terms of performance (actual output) and capacity (potential output) cannot be ignored, and may help to explain many of the puzzling phenomena of hypnosis. It certainly presents a simpler explanation than one in terms of a sudden and mysterious occurrence of greater muscular power.

It is sometimes said that the results from such tests of muscular strength reflect the expectation of the hypnotist. In an unpublished study of this problem, the writer let it be known to members of group A that he expected positive increase of muscular grip ability in hypnosis, to members of group B that he did not, and to members of group C that he was not sure whether or not he would obtain differences. No significant changes in any of the groups were obtained. Perhaps the hypnotist was not positively positive or negatively negative enough!

INCREASED SENSORY ACUITY
(*HYPER*AESTHESIA)

It may be asked whether or not improved sensory ability, such as improved hearing or improved vision, is possible in hypnosis. Objection is again levelled not so much at the reported results of increased acuity as at the failure to differentiate between performance and capacity. In addition such reports, especially those in which increased acuity was claimed, suffer from the defect of the lack of a control group and raise the old question whether or not such increase could have occurred in the normal waking state. It is the writer's belief that a great reserve of potential resides in many of our senses. This reserve is not drawn on for the simple reason that it is not needed; however, if required during the course of hypnotic sessions it may be elicited.

A good example of the fact that the appearance of a new ability in one of the senses need not be an occasion for surprise is the following. The writer was once a subject for an experiment on how totally blind persons avoid obstacles. Obviously the normal-sighted individual sees objects and avoids them. The blind do not see, yet many of them are able to avoid obstacles. Just how they accomplish this was not clear even to them. Supposing now a sighted individual is securely blindfolded, what then? Would he be able to avoid obstacles? This was the nature of the experiment in which the writer was a subject. At first his performance was extremely poor, but within a month he was able, much to his surprise, to 'sense' the presence of obstacles and to avoid them. It was found that he was making use of auditory cues in the form of reflection of sound from the objects (rather large) in his path. In short, the writer was now able to interpret the meaning of the sounds. He had learned to utilize a potential output present in the auditory mechanism. This, for good reason, had not previously been required. Performance, then, at first was low, and later was high and approached capacity. It was for this reason rather than because of some mysterious increase in acuity whereby the auditory nerve 'grew' or could 'hear more'.

It is not surprising, then, that subjects in another experiment were able repeatedly to pick out certain given blank index cards from a group of blank index cards. All index cards have certain blemishes or unevennesses which the motivated subject, whether hypnotized or not, may perceive. In point of fact, in a recent experiment a special frame was constructed in order to conceal the edges of what appeared to be similar (unused) postage stamps. This was done to reduce the number of possible clues. It might be mentioned that the subjects were still able to observe minimal differences. A further example is the case of heightened sensory acuity (heightened ability to interpret) of Helen Keller who is both blind and deaf. A somewhat analogous situation is found in the case of the individual who is near- or far-sighted because of the shape of his eyeball. Such an individual may utilize certain eye muscle exercises and report progress. Such improvement in performance, however, does not reflect a change in the shape of the eyeball, but rather that the training involved has helped the individual interpret images which are not too clear.

INCREASED MEMORY (*HYPER*MNESIA)

Is memory better in or because of hypnosis? This is one of the most frequent questions encountered in addressing a college group. Students in all probability have in mind the possible application of this increased memory to passing examinations. In material which is both non-meaningful and non-emotional, as exemplified by the learning of a series of nonsense syllables, there is no evidence for superior recollection. In meaningful but non-emotional material, as exemplified by prose, there may be better recollection as a result of appropriate suggestion in hypnosis. Of course, the superior memory resulting from hypnosis requires a greater number of hours, those of both the subject and the hypnotist. It could be asked whether the new superiority in recollection is greater than if the subject had himself made use in the non-hypnotized state of the increased number of hours. In addition to this rather arithmetical consideration is the possibility that motivation as a result of hypnosis may well be increased. A further example of the use of hypnosis for recollection involving non-emotional but meaningful material is the case of a dancer. This girl had forgotten a series of movements in a dance performed a year previously. She now wished but was unable to recall the movements. In hypnosis the dance concert and her performance of the previous year were both vividly suggested. It was then indicated that she would see herself perform her dance, and when awakened would recall everything that she had done. In this way the lost material was recovered. Another interesting case involving hypermnesia suggested in hypnosis is described by a prison psychologist. A prisoner had run away from home at an early age because of difficulty with his father. The father had subsequently left the prisoner's mother, and when he died left a sizeable estate. The son who was now a prisoner felt the mother was entitled to the money, but because of the many years that had intervened could remember little other than the fact that his mother was always crying. He had no memory of the town or even the state he had lived in. In hypnosis suggested recall of the name of the town failed. However, memory of a train ride was brought to light. It was then suggested that he would recall the conductor passing through the car and announcing the name of the approaching town. The prisoner subject was able to do this and give the name of a town. Armed with this information as well as the fact that he (the prisoner) recalled the surname of a family living in this town, the psychologist made contact with every such town of this name in the United States (there were six of them), and in this way the correct one was located.

Superior recall of childhood events often of a traumatic nature seems to be consistently reported in the clinical literature, such events being verified as true by an older person or relative. The use of hypermnesia to recall emotional material in clinical work will be discussed later (ch. IX).

The way in which hypermnesia operates is purely speculative; it may be that in the extreme degree of relaxation possible as a result of hypnosis the resistance (chemical?, electrical?) between junctures of nerves in the brain (and there are many) is in some way decreased. Consequent on this, remote memories (supposed to be carried by nerves) find it easier to 'come up' into consciousness:

REGRESSION

Regression (return to an earlier age) is concerned with the possibility of whether in hypnosis one can go back in time five, ten, or twenty days or years in order to uncover events which may be important in the individual's present behaviour but which have happened previously. In practice this is done by progressively suggesting to the individual confusion as to the present day, month, and year, and then by appropriate suggestion attaining a younger age level. By so doing, the possibility of memory at the desired regressed age is increased. Unfortunately many of the experiments concerning regression lack controls, which in this case would require asking non-hypnotized persons to simulate the regressed age suggested. This characteristic of hypnosis may appear spontaneously (for reasons unknown) or may be induced by the clinician. The question arises, how accurate such regression is. A tool for testing this accuracy is mental age, as determined by intelligence tests. Subjects in the waking state are asked to answer intelligence tests as they believe a four-, five-, or six-year-old might reply. This serves as a control for the same task required of each subject in hypnosis when regression to the four-, five-, or six-year-old level has been suggested. Subjects were generally college-age students. If the subject in hypnotic regression not only responds to the intelligence test as a child but also shows other forms of behaviour in keeping with the behaviour of a child, the process is referred to as revivification. In short, revivification involves appropriate childlike behaviour in addition to intellectual regression, and this is considered to constitute a more complete form of regression. Clinically, the results, while not indicating exactness, seem to show the operation of some kind of regression or revivification. Positive results, similar to those for intelligence tests, were found for drawing, handwriting, and other tests in which the performance required could not even be guessed. Frequently, there appears to be a reliving of a past situation in the framework of the present. This is seen by the shifting verb tenses used by the patient undergoing the regression or as it may turn out the revivification. It is customary for the hypnotist to identify himself with some person whom the subject knew at the regressed time. This is done in order that the presence of the hypnotist will not seem incongruous to the regressed subject, inasmuch as the hypnotist represents a figure from a later period in the subject's life. On the one hand, one is impressed by the resurgence of certain early physiological reflexes whose nature is unknown to most individuals (although not all reflexes show an infantile reaction). On the other hand, one is depressed by the ability of a child of six to define words like hypochondria, as well as by the fact that such a child will, when asked the time, look at his wrist! The lack of critical ability on the part of the regressed subject is said to rescue him from the paradox of finding himself in such a situation. Regression thus seems to be a matter of degree.

Regression has unfortunately lent itself to the manipulations of the quack in an ultra-sensationalistic fashion (ch. XII), and even more unfortunately to uncritical beliefs by physicians and dentists. The case of Bridey Murphy illustrates this point carried to an extreme.* Bridey Murphy is the supposed previous incarnation who emerged when 'another person' had been hypnotized and regressed a few hundred years. There have been, and may continue to be, a succession of Bridey Murphys. The present writer was contacted, by a reader of Bernstein's book, and inquiry was made whether I could regress the person to an early age and then leave her there. Questioning brought out the fact that this was a seeing age – she had been stone blind for over forty years! This quasi belief in miracles makes one both mad and sad. Mad that there is no law protecting such individuals from having their hopes raised so futilely; sad that the veneer of scientific thought is so thin.

* The Search for Bridey Murphy, M. Bernstein, New York (Doubleday), 1956; see also A Scientific Report on "The Search for Bridey Murphy", M. Kline (Ed.), New York (Julian Press), 1956.

SPECIAL ABILITIES

In hypnosis can one play the piano or speak a foreign language if these are suggested? The answer to this question is yes – provided one could do so before. People showing a 'new' ability are not necessarily showing it for the first time, but may be showing it (if no trickery is involved) as a result of the removal by hypnosis of an inhibition or block which prevented the appearance of this previously acquired ability. It is not implied that the previous learning is always conscious. A case is cited of a man being able to repeat a passage in an ancient language. He was completely unable to account for this, inasmuch as he had no knowledge whatsoever of the language and could not remember ever having seen the passage. Careful research subsequently disclosed that he had at one time been seated in a library where a book lay open at the passage in question, and that it must have caught his eye and registered in his memory while he was consciously absorbed in thinking about other matters.

In all cases of reported improvement in ability, be it sensory, motor, or memory, four factors must be watched for. Is there a control whereby it is known that the phenomenon being reported could not occur in the waking state? Was the ability ever present in the individual before? Is a differentiation made between potential output and actual output? (It is believed that improved ability is more likely to be shown by those individuals whose performance is significantly lower than their capacity.) Finally, it may be asked whether there is recognition that hypnosis may provide the impetus to use other clues. That hypers do occur is not contested so much as is the interpretation of their meaning. More definitive rather than cautious conclusions would be possible if maximum motivation were obtained for both hypnotized and non-hypnotized states.

Chapter VIII

THE VOLITIONAL AND THE MORAL QUESTION

THE positive use of hypnosis as a therapeutic and research instrument and its negative use for entertainment purposes are recognized. In the present chapter we shall be more concerned with certain of the social problems associated with hypnosis. The problems at issue here are the ones about which people invariably ask whenever the topic of hypnosis is raised. The questions are generally phrased in somewhat the following manner: 'Can a person be hypnotized against his will?' and 'Can a person be made to do anything in hypnosis that *he* would not normally do?' (It is of interest to note that the last question is often put as follows: 'Can a person be made to do anything in hypnosis that *she* wouldn't normally do?') Both questions seem to imply departure from normal or desired behaviour, both involve similar consideration of certain relevant questions, and consequently both are examined in this chapter.

Before going into a more detailed examination of these questions, three points should be kept in mind. In considering the possible answers to these questions, the more obvious *act* rather than the not so obvious *intent* should be given priority. As matters now stand, tests which try to reveal intent need to be much improved if we are to gain insight into the motivations (intent) of man. Acts, on the other hand, represent concrete and observable behaviour. By emphasizing act, issues stay much closer to objective facts rather than to speculation. By analogy we see the problem of act versus intent in clearer perspective when we consider the reaction of nations to legal issues. In times of stress and hysteria, a nation not only emphasizes conformity but frequently tends to change requirements of judicial proof from clear and obvious fact (acts) to preconceived ideas and judgements of what should be (intent). Secondly, the fact that hypnosis has been used as an anaesthetic for major operations (ch. X) would argue for the possibility that hypnosis may achieve ends that are not normally expected. Finally, many of the questions asked are concerned with sex. The reason for this is simple: it is in the area of sex that our culture has the largest number of taboos. Reputed seduction and actual seduction in hypnosis, however, may often be two entirely different things. When claims of seduction in hypnosis have been investigated, it has often been found that either the seduction and/or the hypnosis have been entirely fictional. It should also be realized that hypnosis may serve as a convenient excuse. All this is not to say that seduction in hypnosis is impossible, but that there may be a large number of cases which in no way involve hypnosis.

THE VOLITIONAL QUESTION

The question here is whether a person can be hypnotized against his will. The popular belief is that if one has strong enough will-power or is strongly adverse to being hypnotized, the answer is simply – no. This question, however, is a mass of verbal confusion. What is meant by 'against'? What is meant by 'strongly'? What is meant by 'will-power'? The concept of will is a rather mystical one, and it is nowadays not a respectable psychological term. To circumvent this objection it may be suggested that we substitute for the offending word 'will' the word desire or motivation. But no sooner is this done than the question arises, 'Are you talking about conscious or unconscious desire or motivation?' Furthermore, one finds to one's sorrow and confusion that conscious and unconscious motivation to be hypnotized may be opposite in direction, at the same time in the same individual! Then again one wonders whether we have here some variation of the old statement, 'I am determined, you are stubborn, he is pig-headed', such as 'I am flexible, you are suggestible, he (usually not present) is weak-willed'. One begins to suspect that in the attempt to answer this question concerning volition, conclusions are often arrived at after the facts are first ascertained. For example, if a subject is consciously eager to be hypnotized (and most are) but is not hypnotizable, then the individual is described as consciously willing but unconsciously unwilling. A person who states that he is unwilling to be hypnotized but is found to be hypnotizable by certain techniques is described as consciously unwilling but unconsciously willing. Results are first ascertained in this type of circular reasoning, and then the conclusions are reached. While such a procedure is easy, it is non-scientific. In some of the literature the word secretly is substituted for unconsciously – a difference that make no difference. Obviously what is needed is prediction as to which characteristics of the individual will and which will not be indicators of susceptibility to hypnosis. Such prediction would be far superior to the verbal gymnastics indicated above. Reasoning should always lead to prediction of results, and not back to explanations of data which have already been obtained (ch. III).

The question under consideration also implies the rather obvious but nevertheless practical point that the person to be hypnotized is willing to remain in the same room with the hypnotist. If he were unwilling to stay, he would obviously be a difficult if not an impossible subject to hypnotize. (It is presumed that this is the subject's first attempt to be hypnotized, since if the subject is already known to be susceptible, physical proximity would not be a necessity. A post-hypnotic signal to go into a hypnotic state can be delivered from a distance and still be effective.) Some individuals, for reasons not yet clear, appear to be more susceptible to one technique than to another or to one hypnotist than to another. If, then, the subject is willing to stay in the same room, has the right hypnotist, and is exposed to an appropriate technique, the answer to this question as to whether a person can be hypnotized 'against his will' is a guarded – yes. The following situations illustrate successful hypnosis of unwilling subjects: (1) There are reports of successful hypnosis in a subject who would 'rather have an enema than go to the psychologist's office'. It could probably be said that this person was not willing. (2) There are reports of known hypnotically susceptible subjects being unable to resist performing certain acts suggested by the hypnotist which they had previously determined to resist. The majority had expected to be able to withstand these suggestions. (3) There are reports of a deacon who made a fool of himself during stage hypnosis, and later when no longer hypnotized struck the hypnotist. Saying that the deacon must have had a hidden desire to be an exhibitionist is of little explanatory value and represents a conclusion arrived at after the fact. (4) There is the report of a hypnotized subject who had a lighted cigarette so placed between his interlaced fingers that it would burn them unless he unclasped his hands, as he firmly believed he could. The result of the experiment was the odour of burning flesh. (5) There is the case of a previously hypnotized subject who tried to resist being hypnotized by plugging her ears, closing her eyes, and yelling – but all to no avail. (6) There is the case of the successful hypnotizing of a subject who had lost all faith in life and was resistant to any and all forms of treatment. (7) It is known that the unwilling-to-be-hypnotized subject acting as a 'chaperone' for a friend may be hypnotized. It would clearly be poor logic to state that a person could not be hypnotized 'against his will' if this particular technique had not been utilized in the case of the unwilling person (ch. IX). (8) The reaction of subjects who become hysterical seems to indicate that individuals may be hypnotized even when ostensibly not wishing to be. (9) The use of drugs is said to make an actively resistant person, not otherwise amenable to hypnosis, susceptible. By implication, many of the points raised concerning the moral question are also relevant to the question of volition.

THE MORAL QUESTION

The perennial question as to whether a person in hypnosis (or after hypnosis utilizing a post-hypnotic suggestion) can be made to do anything he or she would not normally do, or which is against his or her 'moral code', has had many answers. There are some investigators in the field of hypnosis who say no, some who say yes, some who believe the question is meaningless, some who do not mean what they say, and some who say that in hypnosis an individual is even more moral than in the waking state. Such answers are generally given quite emphatically. Before discussing this question, it is important to realize that moral principles are not quite so rigid as is often thought. One has only to consider man's behaviour in war to realize that he can be led, or misled, into the act of killing. Or consider the Kinsey data on sexual behaviour. Here practising and preaching seem to be two different matters. Furthermore, there exists a school of thought which believes that almost everyone is potentially capable of anti-social acts, acts which hypnosis may release. Such considerations would or should give one pause before deciding from what 'moral code' of behaviour one is departing.

Those who emphasize the answer 'no' to this moral question cite the case of a girl who, in front of a group of male medical students, showed all the phenomena of the deep hypnotic state. She hallucinated, 'murdered', robbed, but when told to disrobe, abruptly awakened. Such people also tell of the failure of a well-known hypnotist to get his subjects to commit a theft, and of the hypnotized subject who would stab a real man with a rubber knife or a straw man with a real knife, but suddenly came out of the hypnotic state when requested to stab a real man with a real knife. Let us look into some of the factors which should be considered in evaluating these situations which are said to support a 'no' answer to the moral question.

NEGATIVE EVIDENCE

First is the problem of negative data. This is rather succinctly illustrated in a poem by Robert Service. In this poem we are told of a preacher at the front lines who was hit over the heart by a bullet but whose life was saved by a Bible which he conveniently carried in his breast pocket. This is good. You hear much about it. The press reports it. We tell it to our children. This is positive evidence of the value of ethical living. Service then goes on to tell about an inveterate gambler at the front lines who was also hit over the heart by a bullet, but whose life was saved by a pack of cards which he conveniently carried in his breast pocket. This is bad. We seldom hear about it. The press fails to report it. We do not tell it to our children. This is negative evidence of the value of ethical living. Returning to the field of hypnosis, negative evidence for the answer of 'no' to the moral question being considered would be present if it had been reported that the girl had undressed in front of the medical class. But if this had occurred, it may be questioned whether journals or texts would carry this report. Certainly in evaluating data it would be important to generalize from both successful (positive) and unsuccessful (negative) cases.

LOGIC

A second factor to be kept in mind in evaluating the data on this moral question concerns the application of logic. If the girl had undressed before the class (or if any act is performed contrary to the *mores* of the individual), it might well be said that the girl (or the person performing the anti-social act) was basically immoral and that the act in question was not *really* contrary to the person's moral principles or 'fundamental personal character', or again that such an act actually was in conformity with 'innermost desires'. Such reasoning and conclusion is again clearly after the facts and does not involve, as it should, prediction. Still another point in the use of logic is illustrated in the example of the failure to get subjects to rob, which is often given by those who answer 'no' to the moral question. In this case the hypnotist, a competent person, was not able to make his subjects who were in the hypnotic state commit thefts. The reason he advanced as to why others had been successful was that their subjects had been aware of the 'protected' nature of the situation. That is, they knew that they would not actually be requested to do anything outside the pale of reason or to perform any act that would get them into difficulty. However, it would seem that this feeling of being 'protected' would apply equally to all hypnotists, especially when situations similar in all observable respects are deliberately constructed to allow for the possibility of comparing results. One might actually take advantage in a positive sense of the subject's feeling of being protected to accomplish performance of the theft. Furthermore, in those experiments in which the hypnotist did obtain the commission of a theft, why should the subjects, if they understood that the situation was 'protected', have experienced and reported guilt feelings?

METHOD

The question of method is of paramount importance in considering the answer to the moral question. In the example of the girl who was requested to disrobe, proper (improper?) use of method might have enabled the hypnotist to succeed. While no single factor, it is true, can be considered to be *the* factor in eliciting anti-social behaviour, nevertheless the role of method approaches this. Proper usage would involve employment of whatever characteristics of hypnosis seem to be demanded by the situation.

Methods of hypnotic induction may be thought of as including three types. One is characterized by a bare statement to the subject in hypnosis of the end desired. Two is characterized by a full description of even minor details of the situation. Three utilizes the hallucinations possible in hypnosis. Generally no one method is present alone, but one of the three will predominate. In our present state of ignorance, the relative efficacy of any of these methods or combination thereof is open to question. Suppose I wish to make X who is in hypnosis kill a cat. I might simply tell X to kill the cat, thus employing method one, and it might work. However, if I knew that X was an animal lover, method three might be more appropriate. Using this method, X might be told that he would see the cat as a tiger (hallucination), that it was dangerous, that its bite was poisonous resulting in suffering and death, and that it was about to attack him. He would then be told that in self-defence he would shoot the animal. If the details were sufficiently elaborated, it might well be argued that method two had also been involved. Thus, in the situation described (killing a cat) any combination of methods or merely the use of one method alone may be successful. There have been many reports of individuals who were directed to throw sulphuric acid at the experimenter and did so (method one). The destructive properties of sulphuric acid on the skin and eyes had first been indicated. The experimenter, unknown to the subject, was protected by invisible glass (this curved glass acts by cutting out all reflecting rays). That the glass was actually invisible was indicated by other experiments with a large number of non-hypnotized subjects. In point of fact, one researcher changed from answering the moral question from a 'no' to a 'yes' when he succeeded in making a subject throw just such a solution of acid at another individual who in this case was unprotected. Other experiments utilizing invisible glass required individuals in hypnosis to pick up a deadly snake (method one), or they might be told that they would see the snake as a coiled piece of rubber hose (method three), and would pick up the rubber hose. In both cases with either method one or three, the suggestions were successful, and the subjects were only prevented from actually picking up the snake by the presence of invisible glass. It has been said that this experiment succeeded only because the subjects in hypnosis have hyperacuity of vision, and are consequently able to see the invisible glass and to realize that they are not in any imminent danger. Such a conclusion, however, is reached in the absence of, not the presence of, information.

Using methods one and two, a person in hypnosis was directed to reveal knowledge she did not wish to divulge. The procedure in this case was to describe in minute detail how the information was first at the back of the throat, then in the back of the mouth, proceeding along the tongue, at the back of the teeth, at the lips, and so on. The desired information was then described as having literally 'exploded forth'. One experimenter interested in inducing colour-blindness with the subject in a profound hypnotic state found that he could not merely suggest colour-blindness (method one), but in addition to other modifications had to suggest complete blindness, the anxiety that the subject felt on discovering this, and then the possession of limited colour vision (method two). When this was done a type of colour vision possible only to colour-blind and not to normal-sighted individuals was elicited. (What actually happened physiologically is problematical, since little is known about either hypnosis or colour-blindness and an answer in terms of central brain processes explains little if anything.) Another example of the employment of methods one and two is the experiment in which hypnotized medical students were told they had illegally performed an abortion. The hypnotist in this case did not content himself with a flat matter-of-fact statement to the effect, 'You have committed an abortion' (method one), but rather chose to describe in detail (method two) the woman requesting the abortion, her tearful voice, the journey to her house, the flat she lived in, the stairway to the flat, and the details of the operation itself. With this procedure he was able (in nine out of twelve subjects) to suggest the presence of conflict, to induce guilt feelings, and to proceed successfully with the experiment; that is, to obtain in six of his subjects both psychological and physiological disturbances. What results would have been obtained if there had only been a flat statement (method one) can only be guessed. However, on the basis of the fact that another experiment had not succeeded in inducing colour-blindness when a simple statement concerning the end desired was made (method one) but was successful when detailed description was given (method two) may indicate that in this particular experiment success was more likely to occur with a combination of methods one and two. Method three may be employed, as in the hypothetical example of the cat-loving-but-killing subject, by utilizing hallucination.

If confidential material is sought, the hypnotist may, as has been done, suggest that he, the hypnotist, is the subject's superior or confidant. During World War II a high-test petrol was being developed, and the officer in charge of this research was certain that no one on the research team would or could be made to divulge the contents of their findings. The hypnotist to whom this challenge was made proceeded to hypnotize one member of the research group. After the individual had been hypnotized, the hypnotist suggested that he, the hypnotist, was the commanding officer, and asked for briefing on what had transpired. The demonstration had to be stopped before too much confidential information was revealed.

Another instance of success with method three involved the eliciting of sexual fantasies in hypnosis by having the subject hallucinate that he was retiring for the night. These fantasies could not be evoked in the waking state. A further case illustrating the successful application of method three reported a

112

physical attack (which narrowly avoided serious consequences) of one soldier upon another when it was suggested in hypnosis that an enemy soldier was present. The success of these different procedures merely indicates that all methods should be considered before any conclusion is reached concerning the possibility or impossibility of anti-social acts occurring.

In the previous paragraph it was said that before concluding that anti-social acts cannot be caused, consideration should be given to the number of methods which exist and which may induce such acts. In saying this, the danger of reasoning after the fact is recognized. The writer is not stating that negative results are the outcome of poor method, but is claiming that negative results *might* have occurred because of inappropriate method. It is obviously incorrect to say that if one obtains positive results, then the method must have been satisfactory, and vice versa. What is being argued is that we can better understand and predict from the use of different methods than from the subjective moral code of the individual. Conclusive data on the comparative effectiveness of a method or combination of methods, as well as the kinds of individuals on whom these methods are most effective, are still lacking. All that can be said at present is that a variety of methods should be considered and applied.

RESPONSIBILITY

In all methods (and especially with method three where a different intent has been created) the question of responsibility is present. In the example of shooting the cat, it might be asked who is responsible, the person performing the hypnosis (hypnotist) or the person doing the shooting (the hypnotized)? The objective fact is that the cat has been killed, and if the law were to punish for this, in all likelihood the person doing the shooting (the act), that is the hypnotized, would be found guilty, and not the hypnotist who implanted the motive (intent). The qualification 'in all likelihood' is made because a case has been reported in America in which a hypnotized subject who murdered (not responsible but guilty) was freed, while the person doing the hypnosis (responsible but not guilty) was hanged. This, however, is infrequent, and the law usually judges on the basis of act rather than of intent.

CONCLUSION

Returning again to the original example of the girl's undressing, we may now say several things: (1) There may only be a record of positive cases which support a 'no' answer to the question under consideration; in short, negative evidence may have been ignored. (2) The question of whether, if the girl had undressed, she was *really* immoral is impossible to answer and reflects a logical fallacy of reasoning after the facts. (3) The question of method is of considerable importance. Instead of using a direct method of telling the girl to undress, a technique of suggesting to the girl that it is late, that she is tired, that she is alone, that she is preparing to go to bed, and that she will undress for the night, might have been tried. In short, it is being suggested that techniques two or three instead of technique one *might* have obtained results. Certainly before the incident of the girl's failing to undress before a medical group can be cited as an example to support a 'no' answer to this moral question, a variety of methods should be attempted.

At the beginning of this section, three other answers to the moral question besides a yes or no response were described. It was mentioned that certain investigators believe the moral question to be meaningless. They argue that if by hallucination in hypnosis (method three) one can circumvent the question of intent, then in effect there is no moral issue for there is no violation of conscience involved. It should be remembered, however, that there are other methods. A second answer concerns those individuals who are reluctant to discuss this matter of anti-social behaviour publicly, and take a position contrary to what they personally think (believe yes but say no) for fear lest this aspect of hypnotic phenomena jeopardize further work. It can only be said, in regard to this position, that the fact that a procedure is misused or abused is not a legitimate argument against its judicious use. Finally, it has been said that an individual is even more moral in hypnosis. This is an aspect about which there has been little investigation. A case is cited, the only one the writer could find, of a girl who showed increased modesty concerning examination by a physician in the hypnotic state as compared with the waking state.

AN UNFINISHED PROJECT

Related to the volitional and moral question and indicating the effectiveness of hypnosis is the following. The investigation in question occurred some years ago at a large university in the eastern part of the United States. The writer was interested in and wished to experiment with religious belief, but inasmuch as religion was and is considered to be a 'touchy' topic, it was decided to try to change the attitude of a non-believer to belief. In this way it was thought that should the experiment in some way or another come to the attention of the powers that be, promotion instead of demotion might result! A person who may be described as vehemently atheistic and who showed all the phenomena of deep hypnosis was found. The experimenter had intended to give a paper-and-pencil test of attitude to religion both before and after hypnotic suggestion. For reasons to be explained, only the 'before' test was given. The hypnotic subject lived and ate in a boarding-house, and at the same house the writer found a student who was willing to report on the table discussion engaged in by the subject. After the test on attitude to religion had been given, the writer hypnotized the subject and presented him with arguments as to why there should be religious belief. These arguments he proceeded to repeat to the subject in the course of three hypnotic sessions. Much to the astonishment of his eating mates, the subject's table talk concerning religion took an 'about face'. While the experiment promised to have interesting results, it was terminated rather abruptly when the subject, for the first time in his life, started to go to church. The writer had not anticipated this reaction, had no interest in converting the subject, and consequently rehypnotized the individual and told him in hypnosis exactly what had been done and suggested that he would remember everything in the waking state. This unfinished project is suggestive.

There have been enough positive results reported to make one pause before saying that anti-social acts are impossible in hypnosis. The writer would certainly not volunteer for an experiment which blithely assumed a 'no' answer. The question of whether any anti-moral act is to be blamed on the experimenter or on the subject was considered to be a legal rather than a psychological problem, although it was thought that, in terms of the law, the person carrying out the act (the subject) rather than the hypnotist would be found responsible. An obvious and completely realistic experiment resolving any and all difficulties is hard to envisage. Supposing a real gun with real ammunition were given to a hypnotized subject, and he was then instructed to shoot someone and did – what is proved? That the act has been committed is true, but those that answer 'no' as to whether an anti-social act can take place in hypnosis would in all probability now say that the subject had acted because he thought the situation was still protected. To get around this argument – that is, to make the subject realize that he is no longer protected – might require a number of corpses! The answer to the volitional and moral question is best given in terms of the considerations set forth in this chapter.

The problem of whether an individual in hypnosis can be made to commit an act contrary to his or her moral code must be paraphrased to ask whether an individual in hypnosis can be caused to commit an act which is socially and objectively reprehensible. When the question is so phrased, it is the writer's opinion that the answer is – yes.

Chapter IX

HYPNOTHERAPY – 'MENTAL' PROBLEMS

THIS chapter, as the title suggests, will contain descriptions of the use of hypnotic therapy in certain types of mental disturbances. Quotes are placed around the word 'mental' in the chapter heading to indicate that in the middle of the twentieth century we know more about the psychological than about the organic aspects. In the next chapter we shall discuss the use of hypnotic therapy in diseases where we know more about the organic factors than the psychological ones. Undoubtedly psychological and organic factors are both present in most disturbances; the question is usually one of predominance. What a patient desires, when he has a 'mental problem', is help in the form of adequate therapy, not condemning ('It's all in your mind'), nor condoning ('You'll get over it'). While this chapter by no means outlines the fundamentals of therapy, nevertheless in order to understand the role of hypnosis certain problems of therapy must first be understood.

SOME ASPECTS OF THERAPY

CURE AND FAILURE

In reading the literature one might easily get the idea that disease when treated is almost uniformly conquered and that patients live happily ever after. Specification of what is meant by success is not always clear, nor for that matter always given. It should be remembered that certainly in the United States and in some other countries success is important and failure seldom mentioned or reported (failures due to obvious inexperience or to obviously inadequate therapy are assumed not to be involved).

It is important to know what exactly constitutes cure and what failure. This is certainly not agreed upon by all clinicians.

One clinician, or for that matter one hospital, may decide that if the symptoms with which the patient came have abated then cure has resulted. To all intents and purposes, such a definition of cure would involve the lessening or complete cessation of the presenting symptoms. Another interpretation implies that cure is present if the hospitalized person is well enough to return home. Still another clinician or another hospital may decide that cure is present only when the patient once more is able to undertake responsibility for tasks which he had previously performed when well. Between these extremes of definitions of cure, there are many positions that may be held. There is also the rather regrettable fact that if a hospital has a long waiting list, the percentage of cures may suddenly increase so as to allow new patients to enter. A textbook on failures in psychiatry, one of very few known to the writer, has for its contributors top men in their field. These persons spend a good deal of time and pages in this text on failures describing their very many successes, for the idea that we can learn by failures as well as by successes is not very popular. As a consequence of all this, it is not easy to illustrate the problem of failure in hypnosis even though its study may add to our knowledge about the nature of hypnosis and its therapeutic aspects.

What of the obvious, clear-cut, and, one suspects, not too infrequent failures? A case illustrating this point in hypnotherapy involved the use of a post-hypnotic suggestion to combat alcoholism. It was suggested in hypnosis that the smell and taste of alcohol would cause nausea and vomiting. Although this post-hypnotic suggestion worked, the patient circumvented it by alternately drinking and vomiting until the centre in the brain for the latter was fatigued and he was able to drink as he wished. In another case after a deep stage of hypnosis had been successfully induced there was failure to obtain a lessening of symptoms even after what appeared to be important material had come to light. This was found with a person who stuttered. Under the regression and hypermnesia of hypnosis, memory of being accidentally locked up in a large doll's-house was recalled. An intense emotional reaction had accompanied this recall. The incident was ascertained from the parents to have occurred at approximately the age at which the stuttering had commenced – some twelve years previously. Reliving of the situation had not, however, lessened the stuttering. In still another case, the problem presented was that the patient when drunk had a tendency to sign (legitimate) cheques. First there was an unsuccessful attempt to find out why the person was an alcoholic. On the basis of this prior examination, it was said that the patient lacked adequate motivation to be cured. It is important to note just when such a decision is made, before or after the onset of therapy, as this would help to indicate whether the conclusion was based on prediction (before) or was arrived at following the fact (after). In this case it was the latter. Inasmuch as the patient was able to enter a deep hypnotic state, symptom treatment was decided upon. It was suggested to the patient in hypnosis that when he drank his writing arm would be paralysed. This worked. However, the subject proceeded to learn to write with his other hand! The clinician thereupon promptly suggested paralysis of both arms. This worked. The patient now, however, had his friends forge his signature! At this point therapy was abandoned. It could possibly be said about this, and any other failure, that the reason for the symptom (in this case drinking) should have been more skilfully attacked, and that failure to do so resulted in the application of inappropriate therapy. This, however, would be reasoning after the fact in this case of failure Such reasoning as this, when carried to its logical limit, would imply that failure in therapy does not exist, but only failure to use appropriate and adequate therapy. Lest one conclude that such an illogical situation could not possibly exist, consider the situation which actually does exist with regard to psychosis X. This particular psychosis is said to have a good prognosis (outcome); anyone with this disturbance is said to be very likely to recover. If, however, after treatment a patient has not recovered, the therapist decides that what the patient had all the time was not psychosis X but psychosis Y (which has a poorer prognosis). If whenever a patient with psychosis X does not improve, his diagnosis is changed from X to Y, we can never know what the true prognosis of either X or Y may be.

While a more specific definition of cure and failure is needed,

many precautions must be observed in arriving at such a definition. One would have to take into account, in finding therapeutic
success or failure, the problem of euphoria (an unfounded feeling of well-being which may last a few hours or a few days and
generally follows the beginning of therapy in a case which so
far has not responded to any type of treatment; the patient has
often given up or is at the point of giving up hope). Spontaneous
remission (the apparently permanent subsiding of symptoms
for no obvious reason) would also have to be considered. One
would also have to take into account the status of the patient-
in-relation-to-his-complaint. To illustrate, one well-known
therapist had a patient who complained of impotence (inability
to have coitus). One might think that here is a clear-cut case in
which cure or failure may be sharply defined – for after therapy
he either can or cannot. A qualifying feature, however, in arriving at any such clear-cut conclusion was the age of the patient
– seventy-five years! Then again in considering the question of
cure and failure, there is the problem of cure or failure *for
whom* – the patient or the therapist? This is well illustrated in
epilepsy. Treatment may completely eliminate the behaviourally
obvious and subjectively distressing seizures that may accom-
pany epilepsy, but the brain-wave pattern typical of certain
kinds of epilepsy may remain. Has this person been cured or
not? To the patient, yes; to the therapist, yes or no. When
homosexuality was treated by hypnosis some sixty-five years
ago, it was customary to suggest (in hypnosis) an affinity for the
opposite sex and an aversion for the same sex. Case histories
would frequently reveal a change in behaviour but not in what
we now call 'mental set'. Is this cure? A cornet (wind instrument) player developed a muscular spasm in his face when he
started to play. As a result, he could not play the instrument nor
as a consequence earn a living. Since he was leaving for the
other side of the country in a short while, he wished only to be
cured of this symptom – and was. The hypnotherapist successfully transferred the muscular spasm in his face to a muscular
spasm in his left toe. Again one might wonder if this is success
or failure, and for whom? Obviously much depends on definition.

Finally it should be realized that cure may take place for reasons other than those which the therapist assumes to be important ones. Supposing a patient who visits his therapist a few times a week has the habit at each visit of discussing some of his current problems in a chit-chat fashion before traditional therapy is started. Supposing also that some type of cure has been effected – what has caused this? Is it the traditional procedure, or is it the chit-chat or both? In the therapeutic situation there are many factors at work. There is the presence of a sympathetic non-critical listener, there is reassurance, there is discussion and airing of problems that may previously have been bottled up, and many other subtleties of interpersonal relationship that cannot be ignored.

The concept of cure and failure, unless qualified by the idea of goals, tends to suggest an all-or-none situation. Consequent to this, many clinicians choose to speak or write of the degree of amelioration obtained from a given therapy.

FREUD AND HYPNOTHERAPY

The mentor and spirit of many of our present-day practising clinicians is Freud. That he has contributed greatly to our clinical knowledge can in no way be denied. However, it should be remembered that no man is infallible, and to err, at least sometimes, is human, and Freud was human. It is to Freud's great credit that he advanced his theories at a time when the study of behaviour involved everything but the study of behaviour. It was an era of minute examination of the physical organism rather than the study of the total behaviour of the individual.

Freud at first accepted hypnosis as a therapeutic agent, although his later rejection constituted, or so it was said, its death blow. Why did he reject hypnosis? His reasons were: that the cures effected by hypnosis were temporary, that the procedure for inducing hypnosis was laborious, that its applicability was limited, and more importantly (or at least one gets this impression) that Freud had found the mysterious element 'behind hypnosis'. This was – and it seemed to play a large part in his abandoning hypnosis – sex. What had happened, according to

121

Freud in his autobiography, was that a female patient on awakening from the hypnotic state had thrown her arms about him, and at this unpropitious moment a female servant had chanced to enter the room. Inasmuch as Freud was modest, he could not, so he said, attribute this to his own personal charm, and therefore he had no choice but to attribute it to hypnosis. This, then, was the mysterious element whose presence he regarded as sufficient reason for abandoning hypnosis. This is confusing and paradoxical. Freud seems almost to regret the close personal and emotional relationship that occurs between doctor and patient, a phenomenon which he later, although in a somewhat different context, accepts as an essential element of successful psychoanalytic treatment. The other objections that Freud had to the use of hypnotherapy can be dealt with briefly. The transitory nature of cures (assuming some agreement as to what constitutes cure) has been repeated *ad infinitum*, and is often referred to as his chief reason for abandoning hypnosis. Actually relapse into sickness has never been shown to be more or less frequent with hypnotherapy than with other therapies. To the objection that the induction of hypnosis is laborious, it may again be said that hypnotic induction is neither more nor less laborious than other forms of therapy. Furthermore it should be remembered that therapy does not always require a deep hypnotic state. The objection concerning applicability of hypnosis contains a measure of truth. However, no claim is made that therapy is accomplished by hypnosis alone.

One can find justification for almost any position by quoting Freud. This may constitute a criticism, but is more likely a compliment, indicating as it does his willingness to change ideas. Consonant with this diversity of statement by Freud, we find him indicating at one point that his reasons for abandoning hypnosis were because hypnosis, in addition to the points mentioned in the previous paragraph, failed to provide insight into mental problems and covered up any resistance that might be present. It is for these reasons that present-day followers of Freud reject hypnosis. While the validity of the interpretation made by Freud in his time is open to question, the facts available today make it even more debatable. One has, however, a suspicion that hypnosis is currently being rejected not because of the data of research but because Freud said so. His free-association technique which evolved after his work with hypnosis owes much to the latter, for it was developed in large part to break down the amnesia found in hypnosis. It should be mentioned that some twenty years after his abandoning hypnosis Freud raised the possibility of at least using hypnosis as an aid in therapy. It may be that we need a psychoanalysis of current psychoanalytic resistance to the use of hypnosis!

GENERAL COMMENTS

In addition to what has been said, some general points concerning the nature of therapy may briefly be made.

1. Deep hypnosis is *not* always necessary for therapeutic effectiveness.

2. Patients will often go to a physician for an infected toe or an upset stomach before they will see a clinician for an infected or upset mind.

3. Patients often resort to hypnotherapy in a final frantic attempt, a last resort. Consequently, results for this type of patient as compared to patients who come early in the course of disease might well differ.

4. Abrupt or even gradual break through in hypnosis of a patient's defences may give rise to anxiety. Paradoxically, it would seem that the patient wishes to be rid of a symptom yet at the same time appears to defend it by his resistance (forgetting, etc.). Consequent to this, the patient in therapy may give the impression at first of appearing to be worse when problems which bother him come to the surface.

5. Confabulations (untruths) which may occur in hypnosis are thought to be important in the patient's life-history if he, the patient, believes them.

6. The mere induction of hypnosis without suggestion may produce improvement. The fact that the patient feels that finally someone is interested in him and that something is being done may be important. In addition to this, there may unwittingly be some self-suggestion (ch. XIII) during this 'pure' hypnosis.

7. The main difference between psychotherapy and hypno-

therapy is that the latter depends on hypnosis to obtain information. Hypnosis is said to lessen resistance, and thus make available to the clinician data which might otherwise not be accessible, or if accessible might take a long time to elicit. In this way time and money may be saved. One such method is the 'intensification of the mood of the moment'. Here the patient is told that whatever feelings he experiences at the moment will grow stronger and stronger until they are overwhelming. This technique is said to result in the production of data even in non-communicative patients – but it sometimes also produces physical aggression. A knowledge of the psychodynamics of behaviour in addition to a knowledge of hypnosis is mandatory.

8. About one-half of non-hospitalized patients terminate therapy themselves. Some therapists make the gratuituous assumption that this indicates a lack of need for further therapy. While this assumption is nice for the therapist, such a conclusion may be debated. Lack of confidence in the therapist or lack of money might just as well be indicated.

9. Fear of being hypnotized, which to some individuals symbolizes taking a submissive role or accepting authority, may be such that symptoms will sometimes be given up even before hypnotherapy has been attempted.

10. Many widely different systems of therapy appear to have approximately the same percentage of cures. This would suggest that the important factor is not the system's theoretical formulation but rather the relationship between patient and clinician which is common to all systems of therapy. It has not been shown that the strength of the dependency relationship between patient and clinician is any greater in hypnotherapy than in other forms of therapy.

11. The patient may often be able to talk of intimate matters in hypnosis, something he may not be able to do or may be uncomfortable in doing during the non-hypnotized state.

12. Orthodox physicians as a group tend to be indifferent or opposed to suggestion in any form, and think of hypnosis or suggestion as involving deceit (p. 86), that is, as being indirect. While denying suggestion entrance by the front door, physicians often admit it by the back door in the form of pills, medicines,

or bedside manner. Negatively it has been reported that incautious or casual remarks, untimely silence, or vocal inflexion on the part of the examining physician may by suggestion cause or accelerate disease. Awareness of the nature and role of both positive and negative suggestion can only be of value to both patient and therapist.

13. A number of psychiatrists have stated that they do not feel free to employ hypnosis in their practice because of the public's misunderstanding and because of the all too frequent association of hypnosis with theatricals. Misuse has never constituted an argument against proper use.

14. Hypnosis may be thought of as a therapeutic agent in a number of distinct ways: its mere induction without suggestion, though rarely used, may have therapeutic benefits; obtaining of relevant facts may be directly elicited (direct therapy); it may be combined as an adjuvant with other therapeutic procedures (indirect therapy); or finally it may be used to eliminate symptoms (symptom therapy). It is not always easy to differentiate these procedures, as more than one at a time may be involved.

To reiterate, the foregoing should not be considered as constituting in any way a survey of the fundamentals of therapy. What points have been made were advanced in order to allow the reader to evaluate more properly the role of hypnosis.

DIRECT USE OF HYPNOSIS

In the relatively direct method of therapy, the following characteristics are found: hypermnesia (superior recall), regression to an earlier phase of development (often combined with hypermnesia), and post-hypnotic suggestion.

The first case to be described incorporates certain of the above features. It was diagnosed as conversion hysteria, that is the psychological symptoms resulting from a conflict situation manifested themselves as physical symptoms. The case concerns a seaman who had been torpedoed during World War II. The seaman had, among other symptoms, an uncontrollable muscular motion in his arm for which he could give no plausible reason and which had developed shortly after his ship had been sunk. In hypnosis the origin of this muscular action came to light. The sailor had been blown on deck from below, and to give vent to his rage at the aerial attack had searched for a machine-gun to fire back but had not succeeded in finding one. The muscular action of his arm was precisely the motion that would have been involved in firing the machine-gun. In hypnosis, the seaman was allowed to relive the scene, to vent his aggression by firing the gun, and in the process of doing this was observed to release a great deal of emotion. When therapy was terminated and the subject was dehypnotized, the motor symptoms in the arm had ceased. It should be noted that in these cases of symptoms appearing as a result of war the onset is relatively sudden, and this is said to be a good sign for their sudden relief. In civilian life such a situation is not the general rule, and gradualness rather than suddenness is to be expected in both the appearance and disappearance of a symptom.

A second case involved a phobia of the dark (an intense, irrational, and uncontrollable fear). This was painful as well as embarrassing to its possessor, a male of some nineteen years of age. In hypnosis he was directed back (regressed) to the age of three. At this age he recalled, with considerable feeling, being chased by his angry, syphilitic father along a long dark hallway. Permitting the subject to relive this particular incident and allowing him full memory of it in the non-hypnotized state helped to eliminate the phobia. That he had regressed to the age of three was ascertained by the fact that the hallway and the house which he had described in some detail during the hypnotic session was the dwelling in which, according to his aunt, he had lived until shortly before the death of his father. This was when the patient was three years of age. The possibility of a later description of the house being given to the child by the mother is present. This, however, is rather doubtful inasmuch as the mother was reticent to talk about any phase of this particular part of her life. Still another phobia helped by hypnosis concerned fear of being confined (claustrophobia) in a soldier. This occurred as a result of a tank halting just above a slit trench in which the soldier had taken cover. The walls of the trench had then started to crumble, and had nearly buried the soldier.

The third type of case to be described in which hypnosis was of value concerned a boy of some ten years of age who had a continual spasmodic twitching (tic) in his face. It was known that the tic had not been present at the age of nine, and he was consequently regressed to this particular age. When he was slowly brought to his present age it was found that the tic had replaced bedwetting when severe disciplinary action for the latter had been instituted.

Loss of memory, as in the next case, may occur in different degrees. There may be a relatively simple blotting out of relevant memories (amnesia). However, if forgetting occurs to the extent that the person completely forgets his own background and assumes a different mode of life, we refer to this as a divided or multiple personality (a Jekyll-Hyde personality). A case is on record of a patient who in one condition despised the army, enjoyed his dangerous occupation (window washing), was irresponsible, and revelled in drinking. In the other or second condition he liked the army, was fearful of his occupation, had a strong sense of responsibility, and did not care for alcohol. In this type of case, putting together of past and present memories as well as working on current attitudes is said to be of value. Hypnotherapy in this as well as in other cases of a similar nature attempts to synthesize all memory, and by so doing tries to obtain a unified personality.

Can direct suggestion in hypnosis regulate the secretion of the pancreatic gland, the rate of perspiration, or in effect the action of a physiological system? The quiet, sedate situation, most often suggested in hypnosis, may be conducive to the normal functioning of various physiological systems, and in this way, and only in this way, may the apparent control over certain physiological systems be shown. Such an interpretation may explain the reports of success in regulating the secretion of the pancreas. It may also explain the lack of haemorrhaging in dental operations in hypnosis, for it is known that calm (however induced) prohibits or reduces the amount of bleeding even in difficult extractions. Such an explanation rather than the hypnotic command 'secrete' or 'don't bleed' seems to be the answer. When patting a dog, it is not necessary to command it to wag its tail. A control group (ch. III) to see whether command was necessary should be used. In the case of successful hypnotic suggestion of complete anaesthesia, an explanation in terms of calmness, as described above, is of little help. In such a case reliance upon another explanation (though of rather dubious value (ch. XIV)) is made. According to this interpretation, it is said that the possibility of hypnotic commands being effective is in direct proportion to the imagination of the subject to whom these commands are given. Such an explanation while conceivable for anaesthesia, for we can imagine ourselves imagining lack of pain, would be of little value for pancreatic secretion since few people know what it does or what or where it is. Conversely as indicated, an explanation of complete anaesthesia in terms of calmness is not very satisfactory. Both explanations (calmness and imagination) leave something to be desired. A question often asked is whether anaesthesia has to be directly suggested or whether it is a by-product of the hypnotic state. It is not at all obvious that Esdaile in the nineteenth century had specifically suggested anaesthesia. Yet many of his patients reported no pain under surgery. In the twentieth century, however, it is usual to suggest hypnotic anaesthesia intentionally. In comparing anaesthesia as a by-product with anaesthesia directly suggested, it should be recognized that, historically, the methods of hypnotic induction vary, as do the samples of patients involved. In addition the effects of self-hypnosis then, or of potential reinforcement with chemical anaesthesia now, are not known.

INDIRECT USE OF HYPNOSIS

The indirect use of hypnosis as a therapeutic agent in hypno-analysis and in narcohypnoanalysis reveals its role as a helper (adjuvant). Its employment is likened to a chemical catalyst – it accelerates the reaction, in this case the obtaining of data.

128

For hypnoanalysis (sometimes referred to as mental surgery or more generally as a form of hypnotherapy) training in depth of hypnosis is necessary inasmuch as many of the phenomena elicited require that the subject enter a deep state of hypnosis. The depth required depends in part on the severity and number of conflicts present as well as on the therapeutic goal desired. For example, in hypnosis an experimental neurosis may be created. It immediately occurs to one to ask why, if the patient already has one neurosis, should a second neurosis be suggested? The logic of so doing is that the patient by understanding how the experimental neurosis came about may be helped to solve his own neurosis. Creating an experimental neurosis is often resorted to if the therapist feels that the patient is not able to accept the reasons for the appearance of a symptom. The therapeutic value for the patient when he is dehypnotized, with full memory of the experimental neurosis and realizes then how symptoms may develop, is said to be of far greater value than a mere descriptive statement to the same effect. In short, a 'show me' rather than a 'tell me' procedure is held to be more effective.

In hypnoanalysis the clinician may suggest the very activity which in his opinion caused the feelings of guilt and symptoms in the first place. The therapist may then proceed to study the patient's reactions when this is done, not only to confirm his suspicions but to demonstrate to the patient in the non-hypnotic state how feelings and attitudes may sometimes become attached to bodily symptoms. Another indirect application of hypnosis may involve automatic writing (writing without the patient's being fully conscious of doing so). It is often resorted to when resistance or objection to verbalization is encountered in the process of (non-hypnotic) analysis. When resistance occurs, the patient may be placed in hypnosis immediately, and told that his hand will automatically start to write or that he will visualize it doing so. In either case, he is to report what is written. The clinician believes that he may thus side-track resistance. If this is not successful, he may attempt to circumvent resistance by a number of other techniques. One such technique is to have the patient in hypnosis look into a crystal ball or imagined movie screen, and at the same time be told that he will see images or action pertinent to his symptoms, which he is then to describe.

Still another way in which hypnosis may be helpful in this indirect fashion is in the testing of personality resources which the clinician has attempted to build up. In traditional practice, the clinician waits for some everyday occurrence which will serve this purpose. With hypnosis, however, the therapist may actively suggest that the patient encounter just such a situation. Suppose that the clinician is aware that his patient, in riding to work in the morning, meets a certain person who makes unkind and crude remarks about the minority group to which the patient belongs. The patient's reaction in the past has been to become intensely angry inside but overtly to ignore the slur. Now he is told by the therapist that he is able and will express his own beliefs and feelings, and in effect 'tell the person off'. Such a response often starts a benign circle, for the patient is proud of what he now has done, and his confidence is bolstered. This in turn leads to the further possibility of self-expression rather than to the former pattern of bottling-up emotion. In the same way he or any other patient who fails to express himself for fear of getting angry may come to realize that emotion can be displayed without necessarily destroying the emoter.

There are also other uses of hypnoanalysis. The real meaning of dreams may be brought to light, the completion of incomplete dreams may be suggested, or the patient may be told that he will dream of what bothers him most or what he desires most. In doing this it is not necessary to assume that hypnotically induced, and sleep-produced, dreams are the same. Or, again, the clinician may obtain in hypnosis the production of uninhibited dramatics (hypnodrama) which may be revealing of the patient's problems. It is true that such drama may be undertaken in the non-hypnotic state, but its performance in this state is often done with hesitation, awkwardness, and frequently self-consciousness.

In all these ways the therapist may obtain information which is either not ordinarily available or which would take longer to uncover – data which are valuable for therapy. Frequently the clinician, if he believes that memory of the data obtained might be painful in the conscious state, suggests amnesia for the incident uncovered in hypnosis, or may suggest that the person will not consciously remember the material until he is ready to do so. To develop a patient to the point where he will show in hypnosis experimental neurosis, automatic writing, dream completion, and the like requires at least five training sessions of slow systematic induction, each of about two hours in length. Treatment under hypnoanalysis generally is reputed to last about six months with four to five visits per week. Traditional psychoanalysis is said to require about four times as long as this. However, in the light of certain other estimates it is probably safer to say only that hypnoanalysis takes a shorter time to effect its goal than does traditional psychoanalysis.

NARCOHYPNOANALYSIS

In narcoanalysis (not narcohypnoanalysis) does the state produced by drugs actually resemble hypnosis? Is narcoanalysis similar to hypnoanalysis? While the two states appear to be the same and are often used for the same purpose, individuals who have employed both claim that hypnoanalysis produces more vivid emotions and is more sensitive. One fictitious belief, fairly widespread, must first be dealt with, and that is that people under narcosis or in hypnosis will reveal their 'own' personality or their 'true nature'. There is no evidence for this belief.

Disadvantages of narcoanalysis are: it may not be wise from the viewpoint of drug addiction, it may be contraindicated for certain individuals because of prior illnesses or physical disabilities, and finally it may have unfavourable side-effects. In addition to these disadvantages, it should be remembered that some patients have extreme 'needle fear', and that the needle used to inject the drug which produces the hypnotic-like state may have to be kept in the arm in order to maintain the required level of the drug. Such a limitation in the procedure of injection would in turn limit the possibility of emotional expression, since such expression is characterized by being dramatic and active. The need, however, for eliciting such overt expression may be debated. It has been said by a physician that it would be unfortunate if the more mechanical method of drug injection should replace the more delicate psychological method of hypnosis simply because it is easier to wield a needle. Narcoanalysis, however, continues to be employed, and the reasons in addition to the one mentioned above are varied. The training of the average medical practitioner, at least in the United States, emphasizes physical rather than verbal techniques. Narcoanalysis is speedier as compared with hypnoanalysis. Hypnoanalysis is not always appropriate, inasmuch as many patients cannot obtain the depth of hypnosis required by the clinician.

Interestingly enough, the relation between the patient and the individual administering the drugs is said to be important. This suggests that hypnosis and drugs be combined for maximum effect, since they interact. One might thus argue that there is no such thing as narcosis alone but rather that there is always narcohypnoanalysis. The term 'narcohypnoanalysis' refers to the deliberate and conscious use of both drugs and hypnosis. In the first session, drugs are often administered to produce the state which allows for a post-hypnotic suggestion to the effect that in the future the patient will be susceptible to hypnosis. Conversely, hypnosis often serves to reduce the amount of drugs required on the first or on subsequent occasions. If the patient has tremors or agitation which make it difficult for him to relax or if the patient actively resists verbal induction, then both hypnosis and drugs are required. Whether hypnoanalysis, relatively 'pure' narcoanalysis, or the combination of the two as in narcohypnoanalysis will be most effective depends upon the clinician's evaluation of the patient and his symptoms.

While the states produced by hypnosis and by drugs look somewhat similar, it would be poor logic and neurological dogmatism to equate the two. We have some idea as to how a novocain (drug) block works, but not how the verbal statements of hypnosis accomplish the same results.

Many cases include features of both direct and indirect hypnotic therapy. To be described is a case of severe mental illness of a depressed type which involved, among other things,

132

depression, suicidal threats, seclusiveness, and mutism (refusal to talk). Inasmuch as the patient objected to hypnosis and inasmuch as the clinician had decided that this was the therapy of choice, the chaperone technique of induction (p. 58) was decided upon. This technique was successful, and in hypnosis the clinician found that an important factor in the present difficulty of the patient, a young woman, had been the attitude of her dead mother. The mother had imparted certain ideas concerning sex to her then young daughter which may be summed up briefly – all sex is dirty. The mother had died shortly thereafter, and had left her daughter with this unfortunate, though not rare, attitude. Some years later, when the girl was eighteen, a boy had fallen in love with her, had taken her out for a drive, and had professed his love. At this point she became violently nauseated, vomited, and in the course of the next few days developed the symptoms described above. In the hypnotic sessions that followed the therapist identified himself with the mother, and told the patient, among other things, that her mother, had she lived, would have given the patient different ideas (?) concerning the role of sex, consonant with the fact that her daughter was growing up. The procedure also included some of the more traditional concepts of analysis. The employment of different characteristics of both the direct and indirect hypnotic therapy was believed to be important in the successful resolution of the case.

HYPNOSIS AND THE SYMPTOM

Depriving a person of a symptom may have numerous results: it may create new symptoms, it may release a torrent of anxiety and even lead to suicide, it may deprive the person of adequate motivation to inquire further into the why of his symptom, or it may just make the person more comfortable and symptom-free.

The crux of the problem of symptom treatment is whether the symptom is indicative of something else and removal is an error, or whether the decision to remove the symptom is valid and helpful. In discussing this question, terminology which should be neutral suggests that there is always an underlying 'something', for this is the meaning of the word 'symptom'. In short, the term 'symptom' is loaded, and the traditional outlook suggests that where there is smoke there must be fire.

Supposing a person with a chronic severe headache for which there appears to be no obvious reason, as judged by tests and interviews, is relieved of this nagging headache by the direct intervention of hypnosis. If over a period of time it is found that the person develops no other symptoms, has no recurrence of the headaches, and his anxiety level remains approximately the same, it would be said that the therapy had been adequate, and there would be no talk of the danger of symptom treatment. If on the other hand, in the same kind of case, the headache was relieved by hypnosis, but the subject dropped dead shortly thereafter from a tumour of the brain, one would successively be told : that the headache had been due to and signified the presence of a brain tumour, that properly conducted interviews and tests would have revealed the presence of the tumour, that hypnosis had prevented the person from getting adequate help (if there is any), and that the use of hypnosis, in short, represented nothing but symptom treatment. This type of reasoning sounds logical, may be correct, is in the traditional vein – but it is reasoning after the facts, in this case the tumour. There actually are dangers which may be involved in symptom removal when the symptom signifies the presence of some other problem. Consider the case of the individual whose symptom was a stiff and twisted neck. When he had this symptom the individual was placid and calm; when the symptom was removed in hypnosis, tremors, paling, and marked anxiety occurred; when the symptom was returned once more, he again was placid and calm. What is needed is a procedure which will allow one to know whether the symptom does or does not signify the presence of something else. We could then apply more appropriate therapeutic techniques. At the moment little work has been done on differentiating the various kind of symptoms that are present in individuals. There are undoubtedly some symptoms which have underlying causes (traditionally defined) but equally undoubtedly there are symptoms which do not. Differences of opinion may exist as to what kind of symptom is present. One can only say that symptom treatment *may* constitute a problem for the experienced hypnotist. Symptom treatment should not be thought of as occurring only in hypnotherapy, for it presents itself in much of contemporary medical practice. Sometimes the result is good, sometimes indifferent, sometimes bad. The treating of migraine by pills, asthma by sprays and inhalants, or the many treatments of low back pain might all be considered examples of symptom treatment.

What is needed is a more clear-cut differentiation between symptoms and diseases.

Symptom substitution, that is replacing one symptom by another, the other being more socially acceptable, is frequently resorted to when the clinician is not certain of the situation confronting him. Such treatment is also advised when the patient is unwilling to undergo adequate treatment or does not have the personality resources to do so, although it is not too clear when such a situation occurs. It is also believed that the subject's substitute symptom (this may be a stiff wrist or stiff finger in place of a paralysed arm) must satisfy the same need. Unfortunately, this conclusion as to whether the need was satisfied is most often arrived at after therapy is finished and the results known. Symptom substitution may be thought of as a form of hedging in which a new symptom is purposely given because of the belief or fear that the symptom may be serving an end.

FORMS OF THERAPY

Should one resort to symptom removal, symptom substitution, or the more traditional depth technique involving fundamental changes in personality as the appropriate goal of therapy? In deciding this the significance of the symptom to the patient is important in the determination of what therapeutic goal is appropriate. If in answer to this question it is thought feasible to eliminate the symptom without any harm to the patient – that is, without anxiety or other symptoms occurring – this may be accomplished by a frontal attack which includes the possible use of hypnosis (symptom treatment). It is debatable whether in this type of case, where an underlying factor is not deemed to be present, the term symptom is appropriate, for symptom

135

suggests the presence of something else. Symptom treatment, as defined above, when indicated should be arrived at by appropriate prior interviewing and testing. The second form of therapy (symptom substitution) may involve the substitution of a symptom which is less personally distressing and more socially acceptable. The danger in this form of therapy is said to be that by changing the nature of the symptom one may prevent the subject from having adequate motivation to inquire further as to the real reason – if it exists – for the presence of the symptom. In addition, the substitute symptom must be psychologically equivalent to the symptom which it replaces. The third procedure of finding the reason, presuming one exists, for the symptom constitutes the more usual form of treatment (depth therapy). If an underlying reason always exists, then the truth of the criticism of 'chasing symptoms' through treatment is seen, for robbing a person of his defence mechanism, the symptom, can be disastrous.

An example of symptom treatment is the suggesting away in hypnosis of a severe case of nail-biting. This is believed to be permissible, provided that prior testing and interviewing have not suggested any current reason for the existence of this particular symptom. Follow-up for several years had shown no other symptom to have taken its place, nor any manifestation of increased anxiety on the part of the subject. Symptom substitution as a form of therapy may be seen in the case where a muscle spasm of the face was transferred to a muscle spasm in the toe. The third type of therapy, depth therapy, is seen in the removal of the cause of the symptom, when it exists. Obviously if the symptom of alcoholism arose because of certain marital problems, the answer would lie in investigating such marital questions and not merely in eliminating the alcoholism.

Another way of expressing the fact that there are different forms of therapy, each with its own indication as to when it should be used, may be seen in the following. Supposing a patient came to see a clinician with a severe and chronic symptom. The type of therapy, whether symptom removal, symptom substitution, or depth therapy, is not obviously indicated by a statement of the complaint. If it was found on the basis of testing and interviewing that there was some underlying current factor which was of importance (dislike of job), one form of therapy might be applied (depth therapy). If, on the other hand, it was found on the basis of competent testing and interviewing that there was no factor in the patient's present life which seemed to cause the symptom, another form of therapy (symptom treatment) might suggest itself. The concept of symptom without current or obvious cause as we interpret it today is amply implied in the medical and psychological literature. When the situation is not too clear, hedging may suggest the use of symptom substitution. In short, each form of therapy has its own indications as to when it should or should not be applied. In reading the literature concerning the question of therapy, one gets the uncomfortable impression that symptom treatment may be the procedure most frequently selected for those with limited financial means (it is quicker), whereas depth therapy is reserved for those with not so limited finances. The question which type of therapy should be employed, whether symptom removal, symptom substitution, or depth therapy should depend on the clinician's evaluation of the problem presented and of the individual's resources (personal not financial). Symptoms may on the surface appear similar, but may in practice have different origins and be maintained by different dynamic processes.

Symptom treatment may be used along with depth therapy as an adjunct. This is seen in the case of a patient who complained of insomnia. It was believed on the basis of prior testing and interviewing that there existed an underlying conflict – that the insomnia was in the full sense of the word a symptom. However, this insomnia was very severe and prohibited the patient from attending to the therapist. In such a situation removal of the insomnia symptom may be indicated as a necessary precursor of the depth therapy which was to follow and which was intended to probe for the reason for the existence of the symptom. In terminal cases, where death appears inevitable, symptom treatment is justified and often resorted to even when underlying factors are known to be present in order to make the patient more comfortable in his final stages (ch. X).

Chapter X

HYPNOTHERAPY – 'ORGANIC' PROBLEMS

THE purpose of what follows is to give some idea of the role that hypnosis as a therapeutic agent may play in what is usually called an 'organic' or 'physical' disturbance. The previous chapter pointed out that at the moment we appear to know more about the physiology than the psychology of some disturbances and vice versa. Before this topic is elaborated further, a certain number of points must be mentioned in addition to those of the preceding chapter.

If we can set aside the twentieth-century myth that mind and body exist in two separate states, what is said will not sound strange. In effect, what is being claimed is simply that psychological factors may influence physiological factors and vice versa. We are all familiar with the fact that the feeling of grief (psychological) may make one cry (physiological), that a depressed mood (psychological) may have a slowing effect on motor activities (physiological), that ridicule may make one blush, that the sight of a lemon may make one salivate, and so on. We are equally familiar with phrases to be found in our own and in other languages which indicate the same relationship between psychological and physiological factors: 'He gets under my skin', 'He's got cold feet', 'Sick with fear', 'Like pulling teeth', 'Oh my aching back', 'He gives me a pain in the neck', 'I can't swallow that', 'He makes me sick', and many others. In order to illustrate this point, the writer is accustomed to enter his class, to announce that he suspects that members of the class are not keeping up with their assignments, and to state that he would like someone in the class to summarize the chapter assigned for that day. He then looks slowly around the room, apparently about to call on someone. Few students like to summarize, inasmuch as no one likes to risk appearing stupid. Consequently the members of the class look at everything but the lecturer. Later, after this 'demonstration' is over (the lecturer never proceeding beyond the 'about to' phase), the students are asked about their physiological reaction to this psychological situation. Such reactions include 'butterflies in the stomach', 'sweating', 'breathing hard', 'heart speeded up', and so forth.

Who has the disturbance is often said to be as important as the nature of the disturbance itself. This is merely another way of saying that the personality of the individual is significant in the manifestations of any particular disease. If paralytic poliomyelitis (infantile paralysis) were to strike two individuals A and B to approximately the same extent, the resulting reactions would not necessarily be the same. If individual A had throughout his life been a bookworm and B an athlete, certainly the disruption in the psychological life pattern of the latter would be greater, and as a result the symptoms of B might be more pronounced, especially with regard to the depression which might ensue. In short, there is no illness without an attitude towards that illness. This may help to explain why even in certain serious organic diseases there may be some improvement shown when psychotherapy or hypnotherapy is attempted, for while hypnosis cannot restore lost function in an organ wasted by disease, it can inhibit or slow up the progress of such disease by relieving the tension underlying it. The activity of an organ is often given up before the organ disability requires it. For example, a muscular activity (walking) may be given up not so much because of deterioration of the muscles underlying this particular ability, as because of such psychological reasons as despair or frustration.

Complaints as well as cures are often said to be nothing more than the results of 'pure imagination'. If imagination allows limbs to be amputated, teeth to be extracted, as well as tumours removed, all without pain, then the sooner imagination is allowed to become an active factor in the curative process the better. In considering the efficacy of hypnosis, it should be emphasized again that it is usually turned to as a 'last resort' after all other therapies have been tried and have failed. Such a situation is especially true in what appear to be strictly organic problems. As a consequence of this, hypnosis is seldom used when a disturbance is in its beginning stage and when the possibility of cure is greatest.

The ways in which emotion may play an important part are varied: it may contribute in causing a disturbance (ulcers), it may make the manifestations of disturbance more frequent by creating fear of a subsequent attack which in turn is thought to precipitate further attacks (epilepsy), it may contribute an added difficulty in the form of the attitude towards an existing disturbance (hunchback), or any combination of the above.

Can or should a general practitioner be trained in hypnosis? Inasmuch as medicine may depend in part for its efficacy on confidence in it and on the attitude of the patient towards the doctor, it would seem so. The relief of any ailment or complaint is not sufficient scientific evidence for the specific effect of the particular medicine unless it is also shown that the relief is not due to the suggestive factor which begins to operate at the moment when the patient sees the doctor, and which is part and parcel of the medicine. The suggestive factor is often referred to as a placebo. In the case of a medicine, it might be an inactive, harmless, coloured-water solution which in all respects looks like 'real' medicine. The effectiveness of this factor should not be minimized. For example, a pregnant woman whose complaint was vomiting had her nausea cease when she was told that the drug she was about to take would have that effect. Actually she was given a vomit-producing drug! In similar fashion a complaint of constipation was overcome by a constipation-producing drug. A great many physicians seem to be dimly aware of the role of suggestion in their relationship with their patients. Consider, for instance, what might happen to blood pressure if on taking a blood-pressure reading the physician should frown. It has been estimated that about one-half of the patients of a general practitioner have fairly obvious psychological components in their complaints. Therefore any therapeutic procedure should take this fact into consideration and give due attention to psychological aspects. Therapies which do this, and these would include hypnosis, would have a better chance of effecting a cure than those which do not. One drawback for the physician who wishes to employ hypnosis may be the widespread misconceptions concerning it. He will probably encounter faulty notions more often than will the dentist or the university experimenter, because he deals with a broader segment of the general population. One such misconception, among others which need to be eliminated, is the idea that hypnosis represents a one-shot cure-all.

Some physicians indicate that they would enlist the aid of hypnosis except that its tests for susceptibility smack of the stage. Furthermore, if the patient were to prove non-susceptible he, the therapist, would 'lose face'. Suffice it to say that there are techniques and procedures which may be used in the doctor's office whereby the patient may remain completely unaware that hypnosis was ever contemplated, and so even if the patient proves to be non-susceptible no harm is done to the patient-doctor relationship.

Finally it is best to think of disease as dis-ease.

ANAESTHESIA

In anaesthesia we find a highly dramatized use of hypnosis, especially when it replaces chemical anaesthesia. Such cases are blazoned in the press in headlines such as these:

MY OPERATION UNDER HYPNOSIS.
POLIO VICTIM IS HYPNOTIZED TO
GIVE BIRTH.
SEVEN-WEEK HYPNOSIS BANISHES PAIN OF
SEVENTEEN BROKEN BONES.

In the accident referred to in the third headline the seventeen fractures sustained were of the pelvis, ribs, and arms. In this case the hypnotic anaesthesia was, at the beginning, administered every six hours. Throughout the treatment the patient reported that she felt as if she 'was floating on a cloud'. It is true that as a substitute for chemical anaesthesia, hypnosis most clearly illustrates the distinctive feature of transcending (going beyond) the normal capacity of the organism of the individual to withstand pain. In actual practice the substitution of hypnotic anaesthesia for chemical anaesthesia is relatively rare, and represents only one rather infrequent use among many.

Psychological preparation of the patient for major or minor operative procedures is seldom stressed even though proper or improper preparation has an important effect on the amount and the quality of anaesthesia obtained. This fact is not surprising when one considers that anxiety or fear by its physiological action may make increased anaesthetic necessary. Most patients have been found to be fearful of anaesthesia for a variety of reasons: apprehensiveness of losing consciousness, fear that the surgeon may start operating before the anaesthetic has had a chance to be effective, and possibly fear of dying. The effects of proper and improper preparation were interestingly shown in a study in which the anaesthetist purposely reprimanded the patient for being late, kept him waiting, exposed and rattled surgical instruments, and said such things as 'act your age' and 'I'm not going to hurt you'. This poor type of preparation for anaesthesia was contrasted with the situation in which none of the above errors was committed and in which the patient was told about the operation and the anaesthetic when the anxiety would be expected to begin; that is, when the decision to operate was originally made. The results indicate that a smaller amount of anaesthetic was required and a deeper state of insensibility was obtained in the latter situation. While the results are only suggestive since they were obtained with small numbers, they are interesting. Historically, the use of hypnosis as the sole anaesthetic has never flourished because the period of its beginning (1840's) coincided with the inception of more widely utilizable chemical anaesthetics. It used to be thought that the presence of pain was a natural and wise provision of nature, and that the patient (especially in childbirth) was the better for experiencing it. Consequently, attempts to eliminate pain, whether by hypnosis or other means, was considered to be against divine will and unnatural. Furthermore, hypnotic anaesthesia or hypnoanaesthesia, as it is often called, was not considered to be physical in the sense that a liquid was, and consequently was not considered 'real'. Hypnotic anaesthesia has its function, especially as an adjuvant. Before such discussion is gone into, a pertinent question must first be answered.

This question is whether what looks like anaesthesia (loss of general sensitivity) or analgesia (loss of pain sensitivity) is not in reality merely forgetfulness of pain; that is, amnesia. In answering this question, the experience of a physician is cited because it is relevant. This surgeon utilized hypnosis as an anaesthetic before the discovery of chemical anaesthesia. In over 300 major operations, including many amputations, he described an approximately equal number of patients as 'lying like a corpse throughout', as 'having disturbed trances', or as failing to get any benefit whatsoever from the hypnotically induced anaesthesia. The behaviour of the first group is self-explanatory – to all intents and purposes this group reflected a complete absence of pain. The second group, those having disturbed trances sighed and groaned during the operation, but at no time attempted to withdraw or to avoid the cutting point of the scalpel. Their reactions were *without* reference to the pain area. (It might be mentioned that this type of behaviour is also encountered with chemical anaesthetics.) As a sub-type of this class there are descriptions of individuals who in present-day dental operations squirm and groan *with* reference to the pain area, but who later may deny that any pain had been felt. In this type of case, and only this type of case, can the possibility of the presence of amnesia rather than analgesia be entertained. The third group, those who awakened in the midst of an operation, were individuals who obviously received no advantage from the hypnotic state. This clearly would be distressful in either major or minor operations.

It has also been argued that in drug anaesthesia, often referred to as 'true' anaesthesia, the pain signals (nerve impulses) are blocked and do not get as far as the brain itself, whereas in hypnotic anaesthesia the pain signals do get as far as the brain but are ignored by its higher centres. While it is possible that one might conjecture, in terms of the physiological structures that may be involved, different pathways or circuits for the anaesthesia resulting from drugs or from hypnosis, one would have departed from the original aspect of the individual

143

with which we are here concerned – the behaviour which reflects the presence or absence of pain.

Experimentally, absence or diminution of such reactions as heart rate, respiration, sweat, and other such physiological indices of pain have been shown during hypnotic anaesthesia. It has been mentioned that conscious simulation or lack of reaction to pain of these or other indices was not possible, and such attempts at voluntary inhibition of responses to pain do not present a picture resembling the reaction under true hypnotic anaesthesia.

Why use hypnotic anaesthesia in place of chemical anaesthesia? It obviously was of value before chemical anaesthesia was discovered, and is of value when chemical anaesthetics are not available, as happened during World War II in certain prison camps. Advantages for hypnotic anaesthesia reside in the elimination of: post-operative nausea, potentially harmful effects of the narcotic, and patient anxiety. In children especially it may eliminate some of the unfortunate aftermaths of operations, such as fears and nightmares. With certain individuals who, because of prior illnesses or organic defects, cannot be given chemical anaesthesia, its advantage is obvious.

It has, however, many other applications besides replacing chemical anaesthesia. Hypnosis is sometimes used both before and after an operation in which a chemical anaesthetic has been administered. In such a situation, hypnosis may be employed to induce relaxation in order to quell the patient's anxiety and thus reduce the amount of chemical anaesthetic required (balanced anaesthesia). After the operation appropriate post-hypnotic suggestion may serve to lessen if not completely to eliminate post-operative nausea. Its disadvantage lies in the fact that not everyone can avail himself of the anaesthetic qualities of hypnosis. Even if a hundred and one advantages and only one disadvantage for hypnotic anaesthesia are listed and this disadvantage is the possibility of awakening during an operation, then its value is debatable.

As has been described, hypnosis may be used not only to eliminate the pain of a major operation but also to eliminate pain arising from other causes. Here, however, a note of caution is required, for the pain may serve a purpose. While the patient generally desires that pain be eliminated, the clinician may think otherwise. The reason for this is simply that the clinician is interested in finding out what the pain reflects, and the presence of pain, at least in initial stages, may help him to do this. It has been reported that when painful symptoms reflecting other problems have been eliminated (unjustifiable symptom treatment), the patient has developed other symptoms, showed increased anxiety, or even attempted suicide. As a result of all this, many therapists uncertain as to whether they have resolved the problems of the patient have as a safety measure left some residual pain (such residual pain may occur whether the therapist wishes it to or not!). To the average healthy person, a need on the part of some patients for pain or for an unnecessary operation is somewhat surprising. What such pain or operation gratifies is not clear – although there are many theories which speak of the need for pacifying guilt feelings. A case is mentioned of a patient who desired of a psychiatrist not treatment but a certificate of sanity because his surgeon had required this before he would perform a major operation. Inasmuch as this was a rather unusual request, the patient was questioned by the clinician. Under interrogation it was found that this major operation was the fourteenth!

An interesting case involving hypnoanaesthesia concerned its emergency use for a worker who accidentally had a number of steel needles penetrate deeply into one of his forearms. Since the patient had recently eaten a heavy meal, a general anaesthetic could not be considered and a local anaesthetic was not immediately available. Fortunately the patient proved to be an excellent hypnotic subject, and nine steel needles were removed from an eight-inch-long incision in his forearm after 'extensive dissection'. In the approximately two hours that were required for the operation the patient 'kept absolutely still and exhibited complete post-hypnotic amnesia'. A two-and-a-half-hour operation that utilized hypnotic anaesthesia alone and in which a tumour was removed from the lung has been reported. The patient was described as relaxed throughout, and a week later left the hospital in good condition.

Some miscellaneous facts concerning hypnotic anaesthesia may also be mentioned. It has been reported that while anaesthesia for severe and constant pain may be effective during hypnosis, alleviation of such pain by post-hypnotic suggestion is for one reason or another often a failure. This is said to be especially true with severe organic injury, such as damage to the spinal cord or in certain cases of terminal cancer. Also important is the fact that the personal perception of pain may be minimized under stress (war) or maximized under conditions of anxiety (sickness). Not only must the role of pain in the total personality active at the moment be considered, but the cultural milieu in which the person lives must also be evaluated. The perception of pain, to the surprise of many, is much affected by cultural influences.

DENTISTRY

Hypnosis in dentistry is customarily referred to as 'hypnodontics' or 'psychosomatic sleep'. It is in the area of dentistry that hypnosis, judging from the large number of articles and books that have appeared, has found its greatest application. One reason contributing to this wider acceptance may be that the danger of awakening from the hypnotic state is reputed to be less in minor than in major surgery. Hypnosis may serve many other purposes than merely that of being a substitute for chemical anaesthesia in dentistry. If it served that function only, it could properly be relegated to the museum of curiosities. This broader aspect of hypnodontics deserves emphasis, inasmuch as it is not generally realized.

Patients who regularly visit their dentists, at least in the United States, represent a selective sample of the general population, and therefore one has to be cautious in generalizing any findings. They represent a group which is more concerned with their personal appearance as well as with health. They come from the higher income groups (they have to), and are found, as a partial result of this, to have higher intelligence quotients. As a consequence of all this, they may be said to be slightly more susceptible to hypnosis (ch. VI) than individuals in the general population. A pamphlet concerning hypnodontia suggested for the dental waiting-room has such words as: 'armamentarium', 'meticulously', 'bona-fide', 'placated', 'alleviated', 'indulgence', and so on. Knowledge of such words requires at least a high school background.

Dentists have employed suggestion in one form or another for at least the last fifty years, and the first instance of direct suggestion (hypnosis) in dentistry was reported in 1837. Early reports tell of the surprising success attending dental work when unintentionally the gas-mask – minus the gas – was used, or when 'aqua distillata' (distilled water) was purposefully injected instead of an active local anaesthetic (indirect suggestion). Such surprise at positive results is still with us. In dim recognition of the role of suggestion the dentist or the doctor has been advised in various articles to keep his instruments out of sight, to give praise, and to avoid hanging pictures of a doctor at the bedside of a dying patient! Nowadays many dentists are beginning to be aware that in addition to looking into mouths they also have to look into personality.

The dentist often instructs his patients to relax and be calm. Unfortunately, he never tells the patient just how he is supposed to accomplish this. The effect is generally the opposite of that desired, for the tense person often takes this statement as a signal that something is about to occur. This increased tension makes a likelihood of experiencing pain greater, and in this way a vicious circle is set up. Although hypnosis attempts to lessen pain, such pain may serve as a valuable warning, for it may tell us that a tooth must have a cavity present, long before it breaks, crumbles, or rots in the mouth. It is essentially a matter of making the use of hypnosis as a pain reliever more deliberate, more intentional, and more directed to the decrease of unnecessary pain.

Present-day hypnodontia, apart from acting as a substitute for chemical anaesthesia, may serve many purposes. It may calm an apprehensive patient, eradicate fear of the hypodermic needle, eliminate the need of having to abstain from food before dental surgery, aid in keeping the mouth open, obviate any side effects from the drug being administered, eliminate post-opera-

tive nausea, relax the facial muscles, control gagging and salivation, and possibly (though this is debatable) eliminate or reduce
bleeding in order to obtain a clear operative field. If there is to
be a general or a local chemical anaesthetic, employment of
hypnosis may decrease the amount required. In all these ways
reduction in the feeling of pressure on the patient and on the
dentist is accomplished. In addition to these more apparent
points, the dentist may in hypnosis suggest a sense of well-being
as well as a positive attitude on the part of the patient towards
dental appointments. It has even been suggested that the patient
be instructed to tell five other individuals about the benefits that
he has derived from this painless dentistry while in hypnosis.
Such a chain-gain in patients is of a highly dubious ethical
nature. As a replacement *in toto* for chemical anaesthesia, its
disadvantage lies in the fact that only a small percentage of individuals (about ten) is susceptible to the degree required. Some
50 to 75 per cent of patients, however, benefit when it is used
along with, and in order to reduce the amount of, chemical
anaesthetic required. Over seven thousand dental operations in
which hypnosis has played a part have been recorded in recent
years. A dentist well illustrated how hypnosis functioned when
he wrote of another dentist: 'I have been to his office to see a
demonstration of cavity preparation and restorations placed
under hypnosis. The patient was so well trained that I found it
impossible to believe she was hypnotized. However, the drilling
was real enough and her hands and face seemed completely
relaxed all the time. She told me she was a terrible patient
before she came to Dr K.' However, it is only with the use of
hypnotic anaesthesia as a complete substitute for chemical anaesthesia in dental extraction that hypnosis is unfortunately
thought of in the public mind. In earlier times demonstrations
of extraction under hypnosis were actually held in theatres. Extraction in hypnosis, however, as we have said, is only one
function among many (although an important one for patients
who for reasons psychological or physiological cannot receive
the usual chemical anaesthetic). The question as to the proportion of the general population which is sufficiently susceptible
to hypnosis for it to be applicable in dentistry raises the related

question – susceptible for what? Different depths of hypnosis are required for the different purposes which have been described.

A novel and rather interesting benefit of hypnosis is shown in the construction of false teeth for the patient who has been toothless for a considerable length of time. The problem that arises concerns the proper bite; that is, the way in which the upper and lower plates should meet (alignment). This may be discovered by regressing the patient in hypnosis to the time when he had a full set of teeth and asking him to bite. An impression is then taken of the bite at this regressed time. When alignments thus obtained were compared with alignments taken of individuals before their teeth were removed, the validity of this method was shown.

The time required to develop a suitable degree of hypnosis may constitute a disadvantage for the busy dentist. This fact may make the practice of hypnosis more feasible for the beginning dentist whose schedule does not consume all his time. However, whether or not hypnosis is impractical for the busy dentist depends upon the goals being sought.

Possible dangers (ch. XI) must also be considered, for if the dentist, at the same time as he employs hypnosis professionally, also casually eliminates certain personality symptoms 'as a favour', difficulty may be encountered. Such a procedure is specifically prohibited by professional societies concerned with standards of hypnosis in dentistry, for suggesting away a symptom may therapeutically be completely unwise. The occurrence of 'dry mouth' (insatiable thirst and prune-surface appearance of cheek tissue) was reported when the dentist forgot to remove inhibition of salivary flow. The situation when realized was described as promptly and completely corrected. Dentists contemplating the use of hypnosis have been urged to observe the following precautions: they should find out whether their patient is under psychotherapeutic treatment and, if he or she is, obtain the therapist's permission to use hypnosis; they should, if self-hypnosis has been employed, routinely suggest to the patient, at the termination of the dental visits, that he, the patient, will no longer be able to hypnotize himself; and finally, to reiterate, their hypnotic suggestions should only be concerned (as they generally are) with dental and not mental considerations.

There are also problems which lie on the boundary of psychology and dentistry. Consider the problem of the patient who refuses or 'forgets' to wear his dentures. The question is not necessarily simply resolved by telling him in hypnosis to wear them, for he may equate dentures with old age or with his disability. The problem is thus seen to be more complicated than it at first appeared. A case is cited of a young patient who refused to wear teeth straightening braces in order to get even with his mother! In similar fashion Bruxism (teeth grinding) may represent repressed aggression, and difficulty may be encountered if a hypnotic suggestion to cease is the only therapy used.

Additional points that may be mentioned about the use of hypnosis in dentistry are as follows: children are believed to be more susceptible than adults, five or more visits each ranging in length from ten to thirty minutes are often required as preparation for dental work involving extraction or drilling, about 400 dentists are using hypnosis in Canada and the United States, estimates are that about 75 per cent of dental patients can benefit from hypnosis to some degree, and finally that an experienced outsider (if available) may induce the hypnosis.

If one is interested in pursuing the literature on this topic, it should be remembered that dental journals are likely to refer to 'psychosomatic sleep' rather than to hypnotic anaesthesia. This is done, it appears, in the hope that the unfavourable connotation surrounding hypnosis will be avoided and that this in turn will lead to its acceptance by a greater number of patients as well as dentists. One suspects, however, that what hypnosis needs is not so much disguise as re-education of the attitude of the general public. The fact that the word 'sleep' is included in the expression 'psychosomatic sleep' is misleading, for it infers that the theory whereby hypnosis is equated with sleep is the correct one. Such an explanation is by no means accepted by all workers in the field of hypnosis (ch. XIV). In reading hypnodontic literature one is forcefully struck by the wide variety of criteria for hypnotic depth, the lack of statement of just what use of hypnosis is being referred to, and by the loose and interchangeable references to the general terms suggestion and hypnosis. One is never quite sure whether any form of hypnosis is actually involved or not. It has been said that hypnosis would jeopardize the practice of a dentist. The reports both oral and written would seem to indicate otherwise. For it seems that an increase not a decrease of clientèle follows the inauguration of hypnodontia.

It may be said with confidence that employment of hypnosis in dentistry makes the patient more comfortable than he would otherwise be.

Recently the writer together with a dentist attended a sectional meeting of a state dental association. At this meeting teeth were extracted, and they were difficult extractions, without the patients showing any obvious indication of pain. During all this the writer was sitting in the front row, and was in a position, five feet from the patient, to observe any manifestations of tension, in the face, body, or hands. Of the five cases attempted (they were all ascertained by the writer to be strangers to the hypnodontist) two were susceptible, and it was on these two that extractions were made. The figure is impressive, not only because the percentage of susceptibility obtained was in excess of expectation, but also because of the short induction time involved (three to six minutes). Haemorrhage, or bleeding, has long been a moot point in dentistry, and in one of the two cases involving extraction bleeding did not occur. This, to judge from the comments of the many visiting and inspecting dentists, was rather remarkable. However, the writer was told by his dentist friend that in this type of extraction bleeding is not necessarily noticeable. (See also p. 127.) What investigation has been carried out in regard to the relationship between the rate of blood coagulation and suggestion in hypnosis would suggest the absence of any effect of the latter upon the former – at least in normal subjects.

Otherwise the demonstration was unfortunate, for the hypnotist, a reputable dentist of many years' standing, indicated in his lecture that: there are no dangers in the employment of hypnosis, simultaneous administration of drugs need not be considered, the explanation of hypnosis is to be found in any good textbook of physiology, and so on. While the procedure of this hypnodontist merits study, nevertheless in this day and age when the uses of hypnosis in dentistry are said to be broader than merely as a substitute for chemical anaesthesia, the overall effect of this lecture demonstration can only be said to be regrettable. While from a 'show me' angle an impression was made on the attending dentists, neverthless it is the opinion of the writer that these dentists would silently say to themselves 'interesting, but not for me', and consequently would not be apt to utilize hypnosis in their own practice – which was, after all, the point of the meeting. (See also ch. XIII – Training.)

OBSTETRICS (CHILDBIRTH)

Hypnosis in obstetrics is not new, having been reported in the 1870's. Data concerning it are hard to gather because of the suspicion surrounding hypnosis. However, it has been reported that one obstetrician alone performed over 400 deliveries by hypnosis in the last two years. Its use is said to be especially great in Soviet Russia. That suggestion plays a part, especially in the nervous pregnant patient, is apparent. Often the mere physical presence of the obstetrician may, by its reassuring effect, cause a decrease in the frequency of false labour pains or even their complete cessation.

Here again hypnosis may reduce apprehensiveness about the birth process, relieve morning sickness, eliminate backache, decrease constipation, reduce vomiting, secure a greater degree of cooperation from a patient than is possible with drugs, obtain a reduction of some two to four hours of labour time and consequently of maternal exhaustion, lessen the pain of childbirth or sometimes banish it completely, decrease the amount of local or general anaesthetic usually required by from 15 to 20 per cent, act as an anaesthetic by itself, diminish post-childbirth pain and the use of drugs, and in numerous ways ensure a greater degree of safety for both mother and child. A possible disadvantage of hypnosis in obstetrics, as in dentistry, is its lack of general applicability, but again much depends upon the goal sought by the obstetrician. Another conceivable disadvantage might lie in the occurrence of a stillbirth (dead child), which could happen regardless of the type of anaesthetic. The disadvantage would lie in the death's being blamed on the use of hypnosis.

As in dentistry, hypnotic anaesthesia as a complete substitute for chemical anaesthesia is featured in our press, and it is this aspect of hypnotic anaesthesia which is most familiar to the public. Its applicability in obstetrics as in dentistry is broader than merely as a substitute for chemical anaesthesia. Its benefits are certainly not merely confined to the fortunate few who enter deeply into a hypnotic state. It is often the anaesthetic of choice, and it may be the anaesthetic of necessity when contraindications (reasons for not using chemical anaesthesia) are present. In illustration of the last point, it was recently reported that a pregnant mother with spinal polio could neither have a general anaesthetic, because of difficulty in respiration brought about in part by the position of the foetus, nor a local anaesthetic because of fear of spread of the spinal infection. As a consequence of these two situations, hypnotic anaesthesia was used and used successfully.

Again certain general points may be made. Diminution or relief from pain in childbirth may be achieved in light hypnosis. Labour itself has been reported as having been induced by hypnosis. If hypnosis is planned for obstetric purposes, training in hypnosis must begin some three or four months prior to birth. Such training takes approximately seven sessions of thirty minutes each, the number and length of sessions depending on the goal desired. Inasmuch as the expectant female is said to be prone to develop tooth decay (although this is debatable) and therefore may be in need of visiting her dentist, training in hypnosis conceivably may be accomplished in conjunction with such visits. More likely the husband has been trained by the obstetrician to hypnotize his wife or the latter may have been trained to utilize self-hypnosis (ch. XIII). Such procedures are usually resorted to in order to reduce expenses. Such techniques, however, involve the risk that the hypnosis may be used, often

153

dangerously and incorrectly (ch. XI), for other purposes. To counteract this possibility, the obstetrician may, at the beginning of training, give a post-hypnotic suggestion that the effectiveness of the hypnosis, brought on by the husband or by the wife herself, be limited to this particular birth.

Many persons may wonder about the relationship if any of the Read technique (*Childbirth without Fear*) to the use of hypnosis in childbirth. Certainly the thesis that our culture engenders fear about childbirth, and that this in turn results in increased tension and anxiety and thus makes for more sensitivity to pain can be maintained. Any attempt which aims at relieving this anxiety and tension is generally helpful. The Read technique by emphasizing relaxation attempts to do this. While Read himself chose not to refer to waking suggestion as hypnosis, others have described his procedure as waking hypnosis. The difference it would seem is essentially one of terminology. Read appears to believe that hypnosis entails the appearance of sleep, and if this is not present neither is hypnosis (ch. XIV). Another line of evidence which suggests that some form of hypnosis may actually be the critical item in the Read technique is shown by the fact that exercises, prescribed by Read for expectant mothers, do not appear to be essential. It would thus appear that the suggestions given in what is probably a hypnotic state were the important elements. Neither the Read technique nor the use of hypnosis in obstetrics, regardless of whether they are identical or not, promises the absence of pain, but merely its reduction.

When lectures alone are given to prepare the expectant mother for childbirth, much the same results are found as with hypnosis or the Read technique. Such lectures include discussion of the three stages of labour, description of the female genitalia, development of the foetus, the significance and value of 'bearing down', and the positive aspects of motherhood. A mother who has given birth painlessly is usually present and participates in these meetings. A difficulty in comparing results obtained from lectures with those from hypnosis is that some mothers who had attended lectures reported the presence of pain during birth, but said they could now bear it! It is important to have the expectant mother differentiate strong muscular contraction from pain sensations. It may well be that the confusion between work and pain may cause the difficulty indicated in the above evaluation. The aim of all relaxation procedures, whether by hypnosis or by lectures, is to eliminate the pain that accompanies childbirth – but not the work. In addition, it should be realized that the obstetrician may be pitting a few lectures or hypnotic sessions against a lifetime of misinformation. It has been indicated that the reduction in labour time and in the amount of drugs required is about 15 to 20 per cent after the subject has been trained in hypnosis. However, in evaluating the significance of this figure one has to keep in mind that doctors and nurses in a delivery ward are accustomed to dealing with chemically sedated pregnant women. Consequently the remarks and behaviour shown to the expectant female, whether it be in the room, ward, or hall, may at present undo much of the benefit which is to be derived from the training in relaxation. As a result the 15 to 20 per cent figure is minimal. It would follow that the pregnant, hypnotized female should be handled quietly, told exactly what is going on, and not be exposed to the moans and groans of other patients. This, however, is seldom the situation.

ALCOHOLISM

An alcoholic can best be described as the clinician's worst friend. This is probably so not only because of the therapist's failure in this area, but also because of the fact that the alcoholic represents a living testimonial of that failure. Furthermore, should an alcoholic be in treatment he frequently, much to the aggravation of the therapist, 'tests the limits' of the clinician by indulging in heavy drinking bouts after the beginning of therapy. (While on the surface this is discouraging, such an event may herald the beginning of some rapport between the patient and the therapist.) As a consequence of all this, there may be a slight antagonism between therapist and patient during and even before therapy. In this context it is not too surprising then that Alcoholics Anonymous (an organization devoted to helping alcoholics and run by ex-alcoholics) was welcomed by alcoholics, their relatives, and therapists alike. Any shortcomings were overlooked, since Alcoholics Anonymous possessed the time, the energy, the money, and the ex-alcoholics with which to attack the problem. They, it was hoped, would put the lie to the old saying *'Qui a bu boira'* (he who has drunk will drink).

Causes for alcoholism vary, and a person may drink for a number of reasons. He may drink to relieve pain, to assuage loneliness, to compensate for inferiority feelings, to forget unhappiness, to be sociable, to overcome insomnia, and for many other reasons as well as for combinations of such reasons. Or the alcoholic may drink for no apparent or obvious reason – ignorance by patient or by therapist must always be allowed for. Whether or not the person is fully aware of why he drinks is questionable; reasons for so doing may or may not be conscious.

Therapies for alcoholism among the general population and among professional people have been of many kinds. The most common method has been to tell a person to buck up, to have intestinal fortitude, to appeal to his 'better nature', or to expose him to toothy sermons, tears, and shame. Procedures like this are generally dismal failures. More scientific, but how much more successful is questionable, is the attempt to cure the alcoholic by drugs. The effect of the drugs is to make the alcoholic violently sick at the taste or sometimes merely at the smell of alcoholic beverages. The results are often drastic, and it is not by accident that it is popularly known as the 'kill or cure' treatment – though this is somewhat exaggerated.

When hypnosis is resorted to for therapeutic purposes, an attempt is made to get at the underlying reason, if one exists, and to suggest to the drinker by post-hypnotic suggestion that he will not imbibe. Such a suggestion may be to the effect that his drinks will taste terrible, that he will be nauseated by them, or merely that he will not drink in the future. The importance of different therapeutic techniques has been dealt with elsewhere (ch. IX).

Most attempts to deal with alcoholism have stressed that the patient must want to stop drinking. A positive motivation must be present. Inasmuch as Alcoholics Anonymous accept only individuals who show such a positive attitude, this fact may well account for their rather high proportion of successes. This is another way of saying that they have a special sample of alcoholics – those that want to be cured. The patient may simultaneously have both a positive and a negative motivation to be cured. Such seems to be the case of the alcoholic who was threatened by his wife that unless he stopped drinking she would leave him. It turned out, in the course of therapy, that she was the prime reason for his becoming an alcoholic in the first place, and that her threat to leave him was not entirely undesirable. Before leaving the matter of the efficacy of Alcoholics Anonymous, it may be mentioned that they are often, through no fault of their own and with the best of intentions, involved in doing therapy without having adequate preparation.

Theoretically a person completely cured of alcoholism should be able to drink, although there should not now be the need for excessive drinking. The fact that the ex-alcoholic is not supposed to touch a drop may justifiably make one wonder whether it is cure or control that has been instituted. (See also ch. IX – Cure and Failure.)

GYNAECOLOGY (FEMALE DISORDERS)

It has been said that the difficulty is not so much with female troubles as with troubled females. Since emotional factors in this area are rarely recognized, the therapist seldom sees the patient until the disturbance has been present for some time. While the female may complain of pain in the genital area, the reason or reasons may lie elsewhere. The usual treatment, however, is directed to the genital area. That emotional problems (anxiety, fear, etc.) may influence the functioning of the individual's reproductive system is no longer doubted. Hypnosis may control menstruation, either by delaying it for a few days or by causing a period to be skipped. Regulation of this sort is of inestimable value to the concert artist. Reports exist of a single hypnotic session effectively changing a three-week to a regular four-week menstrual cycle. This change had persisted for over two and a half years. Dysmenorrhoea (prolonged and painful menstruation) and amenorrhoea (absence of menstruation) have also been reported as effectively helped by hypnosis. The lack of control of some sort makes one pause in evaluating the data and attributing the cure to hypnosis, for it has been reported that a long-standing case of amenorrhoea was cleared up following a thorough talk with an understanding and sympathetic clinician. A case of leucorrhoea (odoriferous discharge from the vagina and uterus) present for twelve years and resistant to all organic procedures had been reported as successfully treated by suggestion in hypnosis. In all these gynaecological problems technique is important; for example, in dysmenorrhoea it is customary to begin by suggesting the persistence of mild discomfort rather than the complete absence of pain. Is this direct attack on the gynaecological symptom wise, or should some form of depth therapy be attempted? Might not amenorrhoea or dysmenorrhoea merely be symptomatic of the presence of some other problem? It might be, and according to some individuals is. They would claim that amenorrhoea results from a desire to be a male; while dysmenorrhoea results from a desire to avoid sexual intercourse. Consequently traditional therapy by ignoring this possibility may be involved in symptom treatment! The difficulty in knowing exactly when a symptom reflects the presence of some other factor may well be seen in this area. Thus many therapists who talk of the dangers of symptom treatment in 'mental' problems will, without batting an eyelid, engage in symptom treatment in 'organic' problems. It would be safest to ask what role the symptom present played in the life of the patient before deciding on the type of therapy.

EPILEPSY

Hypnosis is subject to present-day popular misconceptions, but so, too, is epilepsy (a Greek word for seizure). This is not too surprising when we consider that historically epilepsy was at one time known as the 'filthy disease' (probably because general muscular imbalance accompanies seizures and there is loss of control of urination and defecation). In times past it was also believed that to avoid contagion it was necessary to spit on the person having this ailment. Misunderstanding is bad enough, but still worse is the fact that many people who have epilepsy believe such untruths to be facts and end up by literally hating themselves. Epilepsy is of many types, ranging from slight muscular movements in the eye region to severe seizures (attacks) involving the entire body in which consciousness may or may not be lost. What is its cause? What is known at present suggests at least three possible contributing and interacting factors: brain damage, physical disorder, and emotional tension. In regard to brain damage, the patient may have been born with it or may have acquired it by accident after or at birth. Physical disorder may result from a disease. Emotional upset may be present in the person's attitudes towards his own illness and towards himself. Therapy may consequently be manifold, and may involve surgery, the use of medicines, psychotherapy, or any combination of these possibilities. It is with the emotional component that hypnosis may be most effective in reducing a factor which contributes to the frequency of seizures in epilepsy. In order to do this, it is first necessary for the therapist to realize what are some of these 'beliefs' held by the epileptic. He, the epileptic, is often convinced that his disease is associated with a certain type of personality (generally unfortunate), that he cannot or should not marry, that if he or she does marry the children from such a union are bound to have epilepsy, that as he grows older the seizures will increase in frequency and he will deteriorate, and finally that nothing can be done about alleviating his illness. Data directly contradict all these notions – there is no epileptic personality, the epileptic can marry, the children of an epileptic are not bound to have epilepsy, as he grows older seizures will in all likelihood lessen, he will not deteriorate, and finally something can be done about epilepsy. An epileptic known to the author had visited a colony of epileptics firmly believing that she would end up there. This is hardly conducive to relaxation. As a result of such varied and unfortunate ideas held by the sufferer concerning his disease, it is small wonder that re-education with or without hypnosis is indicated. With such reorientation of belief and a lessening of tension, seizures may be reduced in frequency or sometimes even completely eliminated.

The underlying brain-wave pattern which usually accompanies epilepsy remains the same even when seizures abate. However, in so far as the patient is concerned, it is the objectively seen and the subjectively felt seizures that are all-important. If seizures are eliminated, does this mean cure? As previously discussed (ch. IX) much depends upon the frame of reference – the patient or the therapist. There have also been reports of successful hypnotic suggestion to the effect that seizures (in non-injury cases) will not occur or that seizures will occur in the relatively safe environment of the clinician's office. This latter situation is especially valuable for the epileptic who has no warning about the onset of a seizure (approximately one-half do not have such a sign, called an aura, which warns of the onset of a seizure).

HICCOUGHS

This distress at first seems to be trivial. It is, for everyone but the acute sufferer. Severe and persistent hiccoughs recurring every two or three seconds are not a laughing matter, and may result in severe loss of weight and even death. The reasons for the occurrence of hiccoughs are not clear, but they are said to have both physiological and psychological aspects. Treatments for this malady are without number (there are said to be over 200) and range from drugs to surgery. When treatments are plentiful, they are often not very successful. It is in this setting that hypnosis has been utilized, and has been found to be effective – in some cases (the reader is again warned that failures are seldom reported). A case is reported of a patient with a terminal or fatal disease who had hiccoughs as an aftermath of an operation. They recurred every two or three seconds, were very distressing, and as a result of these hiccoughs the patient had lost some thirty pounds. Suggestion in hypnosis that the hiccoughs cease succeeded in relieving him after various organic therapies (drugs, inhalations, etc.) had failed. Such success had the effect of making the patient a little more comfortable during his final months. It has also been reported that in a mass attack, through hypnosis, on hiccoughs of eighteen patients, fourteen were permanently relieved (the definition of permanent was not given) in one to ten hypnotic sessions. Hiccoughs in the above cases had been present for from one to more than six days, and in the majority of cases other forms of organic therapy had been attempted without success. Spontaneous cures without any obvious therapy, though not as frequent as those attending the deliberate use of hypnosis, have been known in cases which had persisted for over eight years. At the very least it may be suggested that this painless procedure of attempting to terminate hiccoughs through hypnosis should be attempted.

INSOMNIA

Difficulty in sleeping at night is a common complaint. There are many 'popular' solutions: counting sheep, sleeping-pills, music, pulsating pillows (which emit regular breathing sounds every five seconds) as well as many other highly individualized 'cures'. Such procedures may or may not be successful. Among the sick difficulty in falling asleep is frequently serious. Why not use pills? Inasmuch as progressively larger doses are required, the taking of pills may give rise to taking more pills, and this in turn may give rise in many to fear of drug addiction or in the drug's no longer being effective. While hypnosis is not always successful, it has the advantage of not running the risk of addiction. When hypnosis is used for insomnia, suggestions of relaxation and sleep are made both directly in the hypnotic state and by post-hypnotic suggestion. It was the practice in certain hospitals during World War II to treat insomnia by group hypnosis in the wards at night. By so doing the quantity of drugs needed was considerably reduced, and in some cases eliminated altogether. The case of a former drug addict with insomnia is pertinent. This person for good reason feared taking drugs, yet desperately needed sleep. He was finally treated by hypnosis, with success. Underlying factors which may be responsible for insomnia are varied. Sometimes it was found that the inability to sleep quite paradoxically resulted from a fear of sleep! To illustrate, a married man whose complaint was insomnia revealed in hypnosis that he was afraid of talking in his sleep, and thus revealing certain sexual indiscretions to his wife. In addition, a larger number of insomnia cases are said to result from 'twin-bed trouble', 'double-bed dilemma', or 'marital muddles'! In many instances what is required in treating insomnia is counselling concerning the role of sex in the marriage relationship, or therapy for what on the surface appear to be unrelated problems. Frequently the problems presented by an insomniac are compounded. By this is meant that while the original reason for insomnia may persist, the very fact that there is sleeplessness may give rise to further symptoms, such as anxiety, loss of appetite, etc. A case has been reported of an individual fearing that he would go mad as a result of his insomnia. The picture that the insomniac presents is a confused one, and it is up to the clinician to decide what symptoms are a result of what factors.

CANCER

The inclusion in this discussion of an apparently 'purely' organic illness such as cancer may surprise many. Nevertheless, as has been stated, there cannot be a disease without some attitude towards it, and cancer is no exception. In this disease the most important function of hypnosis is to relieve pain when it is present and to make the patient more comfortable. Reports of successful lessening of pain by hypnotic anaesthesia when drugs have been found to be of little value have been made for many kinds of cancer (breast, uterus, stomach, etc.). Advantages for the use of hypnosis in cancer are said to reside in its lessening drug intake, relieving pain, alleviating depression, prolonging life, and making death, if it occurs, easier. That the alleviation of pain was due to hypnotic anaesthesia rather than to the ups and downs of the disease itself was shown by recurrence of the pain when hypnosis was suddenly withdrawn. In cases where the cancer is widespread (although pain is not a direct function of this) and there is extensive proliferation (growing) of cancer cells, claims for successful hypnotic alleviation of pain are very conservative. Here the extreme pain, the fear of death, and the distressed mind seem to make not only the induction of hypnosis difficult if not impossible, but to decrease its effectiveness as a pain alleviator. However, regardless of the severity of the cancer, hypnotic anaesthesia is indicated for at least a trial before 'destructive surgery' (brain surgery) is used. It has been said, and by a physician, that in severe cases it is still better to keep the patient until death a rational human being rather than a 'vegetating' invalid.

DERMATOLOGY

Hypnosis has been particularly effective in clearing up certain conditions of the skin. Warts, for which there are many popular home remedies, seem, on the basis of cases reported, to be particularly amenable to permanent elimination by hypnotic suggestion. Furthermore, from a cosmetic point of view use of hypnosis leaves no scar, as do some cauterization (removal by burning) procedures. Hypnosis is also useful in reducing the itching of certain types of eczema. Frequently anxiety about physical appearance is present in skin problems, and hypnosis by allaying the anxiety may be helpful in eliminating or reducing the severity of the condition. It is seldom that the anxiety about appearance causes the skin condition to occur. Generally what happens is that the anxiety occurs as a result, not as a cause, of the skin condition. The presence of anxiety, however, may cause the skin condition to worsen.

There have been a few cases of great emotional upset (believing one was about to be shot) apparently causing a skin condition in a person who had no previous history of this type of upset. Such an incident is more the exception than the rule. There have been reports of visible stigmata often in the form of skin blisters occurring in non-hypnotic situations (psychoanalytic sessions). One such report described the appearance of skin blisters on the body and hands of a person undergoing analysis when the latter described the whipping to death of her brother in a Nazi prison camp.

The occurrence of skin blisters or welts in certain individuals is related in an interesting way to the matter of individual differences. We may know of individuals who have 'photographic skin'; that is, they show the mark for some time of whatever is impressed even lightly on their skin. Another element that may be important in blister or welt formation is the degree of feeling (in the sense of skin-feeling) that a person possesses. Thus, if one were to describe in lurid detail the lancing of a boil – how the surgical knife is used to cut to the bone and the accumulated pus is then allowed to slowly *o-o-z-e* out, some people will subjectively experience and objectively show some form of withdrawal, while others will experience no such reaction. Possibly when 'photographic skin', the required type of 'feeling', and hypnosis are combined, skin welts or blisters may be produced. Experimentally the problem has suffered from lack of numbers, and in addition one has to be careful lest the subject produces the blisters by imperceptibly rubbing the suggested spot. Furthermore blisters, when they do occur, do not always occur at the designated spot. Results to date seem to indicate that the answer to the question whether skin blisters can be produced by hypnosis is a faint 'yes'.

PEPTIC ULCERS

Hypnotic treatment of stomach ulcers is suggestive and provocative, suggestive because the experiment about to be described is small in numbers, provocative because of the nature of the results. The members of the two groups reported on had all been diagnosed by X-ray as peptic ulcer cases. The ulcers were said to be moderately severe and to have persisted for at least six years. The ten members of the experimental group were given the hypnotic suggestion of relaxation (depth of hypnosis was not specified) and taught self-hypnosis (ch. XIII). Suggestions of relaxation were given during a total of some fifteen sessions each one hour in length. The ten members of the control group were similar to the experimental group in age, socio-economic background, religion, etc. They varied from the experimental group in two respects; they were not hypnotized and given the suggestion of relaxation, and they continued to receive pharmacological treatment. A few months after the termination of the experiment, three X-ray specialists compared the before and after X-rays of patients coming from both the experimental and the control groups. Without knowing to which group any particular patient belonged, they judged twelve individuals to have shown what they termed marked improvement. Eight of these came from the experimental group, four from the control group. Evaluation by the patient in terms of subjective reaction (how he felt) showed an even greater difference in favour of the experimental group. It is unfortunate in this experiment that the control group was not individually seen and talked to about the weather or gardening or in short anything but relaxation, for it might conceivably be argued that the attention received or a combination of this and hypnosis rather than the hypnosis alone affected the improvement in the ulcer condition of those in the experimental group. Results to date are interesting and further follow-up has been promised.

If operative procedure for an ulcer condition has to be resorted to, an aftermath that may occur is nausea and aversion to food. In this situation hypnosis may be of value in eliminating or decreasing this aversion. Results to date while interesting are only suggestive.

MISCELLANEOUS CONDITIONS

Hypnosis may be used in some cases for the relief of headaches, although there are many kinds: sick headaches, tension headaches, menstrual headaches, eye-fatigue headaches, migraine headaches, to mention but a few. As might be expected, with a multitude of types there exist many reasons for their occurrence and many therapies for their hoped-for elimination – of which hypnosis is but one. Reports exist about the successful eradication in hypnosis of headaches which have persisted for many years. Some of these have been followed for some three to fourteen years after the termination of therapy, and were described as being without recurrence and without substitution of other symptoms. One of the reasons why hypnosis may be effective in the relief of headaches is that by its use the fear of subsequent headaches may be lessened – a fear which previously had ensured the recurrence of further headaches.

Nail-biting which involves more than cosmetic problems and where finger ends are red, raw, and bloody has responded to suggestion in hypnosis. Such results, while by no means one hundred per cent successful (no therapy is), and often lacking in follow-up and control, indicate that hypnosis may be of value. Again hypnosis should at least be attempted.

It has been claimed that sex problems involving homosexuality, impotence, frigidity, exhibitionism, and the like have been treated by hypnosis, but here the danger in symptom treatment appears most obvious. It seems extremely unlikely and debatable that homosexuality is, as has been said by a medical man, 'merely a foolish idea'. Sex deviations, at least in Western culture, usually reflect the presence of other difficulties, and their origins represent a separate problem. Hypnosis, when applied to such problems, usually functions as an adjuvant.

Complexly integrated with the scalpel, the dental drill, and medicines is the proper use of hypnosis. It is important in therapy.

Chapter XI

DANGERS – FICTIONAL AND REAL

ARE there any dangers involved in the use of hypnosis? One well-known and experienced hypnotist regretted that the dangers were not more numerous and more obvious, for then he believed there would be less tinkering with hypnosis by the inexperienced. Of course, what dangers there are would be better understood if failures as well as successes with hypnosis were reported. Possible dangers do reside in such problems as the production of catalepsy (ch. V) and in the moral issue (ch. VIII). The dangers to be discussed here are twofold – fictional and real. The latter may be further divided into real dangers encountered by the inexperienced and real dangers encountered by the experienced. Needless to say, dangers for the experienced are also dangers for the inexperienced.

FICTIONAL DANGERS

What are some of the fictional dangers? It has been said that continual subjection to hypnosis (whatever this means) would make one weak-minded or at least emotionally unstable. As has been shown, no evidence whatsoever has been found to support this point of view. Individuals who have been deeply hypnotized over 500 times have shown no harmful effects as a consequence of their repeated hypnotic experiences. Admittedly this last statement is based on a few cases only, for not many individuals have been hypnotized more than 500 times. In science, however, it is generally up to those who maintain that harmful effects follow too much hypnosis to prove their point. Another imagined danger runs somewhat as follows: suppose an individual is hypnotized and then the hypnotist, without dehypnotizing the subject, leaves for some far-away place – what then? Will the subject remain for ever in a hypnotized state? Although we have all met people who look as if this had happened to them, the answer is no. Individuals who have been hypnotized and then left alone tend to awaken spontaneously within twelve hours (the time seems to be a function of the individual rather than of the hypnotist). A press report in England (1949) described the case of a girl reputed to have been unable to awaken from hypnosis for over two weeks. According to the papers, we are told at one point that the affected subject was a ten-year-old girl and at another point in the same paragraph that she collapsed while 'at work'. Such incongruities make one wonder how much, if any, resemblance there was between the facts as they occurred and the facts as they were recorded by the press. The important thing about such a release is that it is this type of press report that bombards the public and is considered 'newsworthy'. Another fictional belief repeatedly encountered is that the hypnotized person is in danger of remaining dependent upon or under the influence (Svengali-like) of the hypnotist. Again there is lack of any evidence. Similarly there is an absence of any data to support the idea that after hypnosis one must feel tired or mentally upset. Three final fictional dangers may be mentioned. The first concerns the danger of inactivating the lungs by accidentally collapsing them in hypnosis! The second danger, more often mentioned in the past but still prevailing in the present, is perpetuated in popular hypnotic literature. It derives from the notion that to excite clear-cut manifestations in any physiological system one must put one's finger near the manifestation centre of that organ in the head. Knowledge of the head areas occupied by the different organs may be gained by consulting a phrenological (bump-reading) chart. The horrendous danger arises when, for instance, one wishes to excite the organ of 'goodness', miscalculates a little, and places his finger on the area occupied by 'amativeness' – an organ of our 'lower nature'! Finally, this author was recently the recipient of a dire warning from a not unknown group. He had failed, it was said, to differentiate the dense, the desire, and the vital body. He had also ignored the deleterious effect of hypnosis 'the greatest crime on earth' on the medulla oblongata of the brain. As a consequence, he and other hypnotists would 'pay for their crime', if not in this life then in a later one, by 'congenital idiocy'.

REAL DANGERS

THE INEXPERIENCED HYPNOTIST

What are some of the real dangers for the inexperienced hypnotist, the would-be life of the party, or the stage hypnotist? In the excitement as well as the confusion of the first attempt at hypnosis, the novice may forget to take out suggestions which he has given. The stage hypnotist may commit the same error. This may or may not (why one or the other is not too clear) result in the appearance of symptoms, the kind depending upon the suggestion that was made. It is wise and a standard procedure among experienced hypnotists to remove whatever suggestions have been given. A few examples indicate the wisdom of such a procedure.

Late one night the writer received a phone call from an unwise and rather anxious student. This person had hypnotized an equally unwise fellow student, and in hypnosis it had been suggested to the fellow student that he was drowning. Later the subject was awakened, but the amateur hypnotist, attempting hypnosis for the first time, had forgotten to remove the suggestion of drowning. The subject had awakened with loud rasping and gasping breathing (quite similar, it was found out later, to his reaction when it had been suggested in hypnosis that he was drowning). The would-be hypnotist was at a loss as to what he should do, and both he and the subject were scared. These, then, were the facts which had resulted in the phone call. Subsequent events involved the writer's going over to the victim's house, rehypnotizing him, and suggesting that actually he had swum ashore and had escaped – the suggestion of drowning was in effect removed. There then followed suggestions of complete relaxation and calmness. With this procedure a cessation of the gasping and laboured breathing resulted. Another example may also be given. It was reported that a patient had visited a clinician with the complaint of a feeling of being followed. This could be an ominous sign of the beginning of a serious mental illness; there were, however, no other symptoms present. During the course of many interviews it turned out that the symptom which had appeared rather suddenly occurred shortly after the patient had been a volunteer for a demonstration of stage hypnosis. The sole intent of this, as is the case with most if not all popular demonstrations, had been amusement. In order to entertain the audience, the subject in hypnosis had been told by the stage hypnotist that he was being chased by a fierce dog. As a result of this suggestion he had run wildly about the stage pursued by a hallucinated fierce dog – much to everyone's hilarity. Unfortunately for the patient the stage hypnotist had neglected to remove the suggestion, with the subsequent chain of events described above.

Sad to relate, there are many other examples. One subject who received therapy for a profound depression of unknown origin was found to have been a subject for a demonstration in which she was given the suggestion, not subsequently removed, that she would be very sad and cry for her mother. As a result of this she had later, after the hypnotic session, developed severe intestinal and emotional upsets, and feared she was about to lose her mind. Such proposals as 'You will feel sad because your little girl has recently died' may often border on the sadistic. Suggestions like this are likely to continue until there is legislation prohibiting them.

If a subject for hypnosis resists, or does not carry out, a post-hypnotic suggestion, it is incorrectly assumed by the inexperienced hypnotist that the subject was completely awake and in no sense hypnotized, and since the suggestion is without effect there is no need to retract it. This conclusion does not follow. It is wise to remember the different degrees of depth possible within hypnosis, and that the absence of post-hypnotic amnesia does not necessarily indicate absence of a hypnotic state.

Another danger for the inexperienced hypnotist is the failure to realize that the subject responds physiologically as well as psychologically to the suggestion and not to the concrete physical reality. For example, a person with a 'weak' heart may be told that he is hanging by a rope some 10,000 feet over a chasm, that his strength is gradually ebbing, that his grip on the rope is slowly giving way, and that he is about to hurtle down and be mangled on the rocks below. In reality, the concrete physical situation may merely involve the subject's falling from a chair to a cushion on the floor some eighteen inches away. Here the important thing to realize is that the subject may respond to the suggestion that he is falling some 10,000 feet, not to the reality of falling eighteen inches. His heart reacts as though he were falling this much greater distance. This suggested situation may be disastrous, and may put too great a strain on the heart – especially if it is 'weak'. An approach to understanding this situation may be seen by considering the following childhood prank, often included as part of fraternity initiations. The victim is asked to step on to a plank, at either end of which stands a person. The subject is securely blindfolded and told to balance himself by placing his hands on the head of a third person standing directly in front of him. The trick is now ready to proceed. The individuals at either end lift the board upon which the victim is standing about one or two inches from the ground while at the same time the third individual, who is standing directly in front of the subject, sinks slowly to the ground by bending his knees. The luckless blindfolded subject will have the illusion of being lifted into the air some four or five feet. When the supporting head of the individual in front of him, on which he has been balancing, is suddenly yanked away and he is left unsupported at this seemingly great height, he reacts rather dramatically, to say the least.

There are many other situations where inexperience leads to danger. The inexperienced hypnotist may by probing or by attempting to bring the subject back in years (regression) release considerable repressed emotional material. He may be panicked by violent display of emotion, whereas the experienced hypnotist may welcome this as a good omen. Coping with such problems is beyond the training and capacity of the inexperienced hypnotist. Anxiety or turbulent emotion is easily aroused in some individuals, a fact that is often overlooked by inexperienced hypnotists. Another danger may be the unlooked-for precipitation of a trance state which occurs because the post-hypnotic signal suggested by the inexperienced hypnotist is too simple and may inadvertently be given. Should the inexperienced hypnotist encounter difficulty in arousing a hypnotized person, he may unwisely and in fright send for a physician, who may know nothing about the nature of hypnosis. The effect of such a visit is often unfortunate for all concerned. There are, in addition, a number of other details that the inexperienced hypnotist is likely to overlook. Has he protected the susceptible individual by indicating in hypnosis that no one, unless properly qualified, could hypnotize him? Has he protected the deeply susceptible person by telling him in hypnosis that he will never lapse into a hypnotic state by himself? Has he made sure when he awakens the subject or patient from the hypnotic state that the person is fully awake before he leaves the office or laboratory? True these are only details, but they may be important – especially to the subject.

The following may constitute dangers for the experienced, but are far more likely to be problems for the inexperienced.

The chief characteristic of hysteria is uncontrolled and generalized sobbing, crying, or laughing – generally a mixture of all three. It may occur when the subject is neither fully in hypnosis nor fully in a non-hypnotic state. In such a situation the subject is unable to carry out completely or to resist completely any given suggestion. He may, for example, be unable to open his eyes, but at the same time he is unable to relax completely. Finding his action not totally under his own control may be frightening, and it is believed that in such a situation hysteria develops. Such at least is the interpretation of the writer based on interviews with subjects who have become hysterical during an attempt at hypnotic induction. What can be done when hysteria occurs? Where only one individual is being hypnotized, reassurance should be emphasized and further induction should not be attempted. If it appears during group hypnosis it is wise to remove the hysterical subject from the room, for hysteria can be contagious. Once out of the room, the hysterical subject may be reassured and calmed. The inexperienced hypnotist may be at a loss as to what to do. It has been reported in the press that a stage hypnotist performing for entertainment (and for money) put on a show for the principal of a Philadelphia high school. Hysteria resulted, then spread, and soon over thirty students had collapsed and a doctor had to be summoned!

Confabulation (wishful thinking, deceit, or lying) intentional or unintentional is another possible danger. Supposing a female subject is hypnotized by a male, is deeply susceptible, and has amnesia for all events which have transpired in hypnosis. In such a situation wishful thinking may take place, and the hypnotist may find himself charged with anything from un-ethical conduct to seduction. It is important to realize that a patient or subject often does not, will not, or cannot differentiate between the sexual fantasies (heterosexual or homosexual) that may occur in hypnosis and the events of everyday life. Many experienced hypnotists are aware of such possibilities and have obtained 'blackmail' insurance (ch. XIII). Others make certain a third party is present during hypnosis, and still others have refused to use women subjects in hypnotic experiments.

Difficulty in awakening the subject (ch. IV) or in keeping the subject awake may present another problem, although there is a difference of opinion as to how common this danger is.

Still another problem, believed to be rare and never en-countered by the present writer but mentioned in the literature, is the spontaneous appearance, for no ascertainable reason, of certain difficulties in speech (mutism), vision (blindness), and the like. All such difficulties, while temporary in nature and responding well to therapy, may be anxiety-provoking for both the subject and the hypnotist.

THE EXPERIENCED HYPNOTIST

Are there any obvious dangers for the experienced hypnotist? Apart from the possibilities described in the preceding para-graphs, it may be debated whether such dangers do exist. Often what one calls a danger may be nothing more than a difference of opinion (ch. IX – Forms of Therapy). It is conceivable that should the experienced hypnotist decide upon the use of hypnotic anaesthesia and have the patient awaken from the

173

hypnotic state in the middle of the operation, this would constitute a danger. However, as has been discussed elsewhere, this is infrequent or is seldom reported. It is also imaginable that the development of an exaggerated feeling of power in the hypnotist (Messiah complex) might constitute a danger for the experienced hypnotist.

AN UNUSUAL INCIDENT

The following incident happened to the writer when he was in the midst of an experiment. What took place was as follows: an extremely competent but plain-looking girl, who will be called A, had been supervised by the writer in hypnotic work, and then allowed to carry out such work alone. One of the subjects in this experiment who showed all the phenomena of deep hypnosis, including post-hypnotic amnesia, was an extremely good-looking girl who was popular with the opposite sex. This subject will be known as B. On one occasion, as happens sometimes for reasons largely inexplicable, her usual post-hypnotic amnesia was absent and she remembered everything that had transpired. It was this event which brought B in great anger to the writer. The story, as she told it, was as follows: A, the plain-looking girl, had given B, the good-looking girl, a post-hypnotic suggestion to the effect that whenever B went out on a date she would also get a date for A. In short they would double date. B had done this thinking that she was doing it of her own accord in order to get better acquainted with A with whom she was working (as has been noted (ch. V), this tendency to give reasons for one's behaviour, to rationalize, is quite typical of the reaction to post-hypnotic suggestion). To make a long story short, the hypnotic work of A with B was abruptly terminated by the writer. If B had not felt free to bring this matter to the attention of the writer, it might have had unpleasant consequences.

Chapter XII
HYPNOSIS AND QUACKERY

'MODERN hypnosis, the supreme power that carries you into a new world. A world of better understanding, of better conditions, of bigger opportunities. By far the greatest, broadest, most comprehensive classroom course ever presented to aspiring people earnestly desiring increased power, knowledge, health, or more congenial better paid employment.' If this kind of advertisement does not obviously remind one of a circus sideshow barker, then it may sound a little awe-inspiring and make one think that if he does not take advantage of this 'once in a lifetime golden opportunity', he is all kinds of a fool – generally he is if he does. Hypnosis historically and today lends itself to many illegitimate ends.

It is true that many erroneous beliefs about hypnosis have been held in the past. What is lamentable is that such beliefs should persist into the present. This persistence is in part due to the simple fact that there is monetary profit in making the hypnotic volunteer appear ridiculous and in thus amusing an audience. Misuse, abuse, or even disuse impede both the legitimate application of hypnosis and the obtaining of scientific knowledge. This is not to say that hypnosis is indispensable (few things are). It is a legitimate behavioural phenomenon which should be studied. Unfortunately both the professional and the general public are suspicious of the topic and of the experimenter. Aiding and abetting this regrettable situation, though possibly not intentionally, are the policies of many well-known American magazines. One such periodical which deals with various phases of life and has one of the largest circulations in the United States became interested in the problem of medical hypnosis. The periodical, however, rapidly lost interest when the cooperation of a certain physician was refused because he felt that their portrayal of hypnotic uses was too sensationalistic, and he suggested a more conservative and realistic approach. Subsequently, the magazine obtained the cooperation of a 'stage hypnotist', and sensationalized the stunt and the stare of parlour and stage hypnosis. Other prominent as well as less prominent publications and pamphlets carry advertisements, not only of how to learn the 'mysterious' art of hypnosis, but how to use it profitably! While hypnosis may need publicity, it does not need publicity of this type.

THE 'WANTOS'

A common factor which runs through all advertising 'come-ons' concerning hypnosis is the endless series of promises. Want to – 'make the weak as strong as a lion'? Want to – 'make the bully timid'? Want to – 'make fun by the hour'? Want to – 'be popular with the opposite sex'? Want to – 'improve your personality'? Want to – 'command others'? 'Want to – *ad nauseum*.

SEX

Sex in and of itself is not necessarily a problem. Rather it is the conflict between the biological *do* and the cultural *don't* which creates the difficulty. Such antagonism or conflict between organic drive and legal taboo does not necessarily result in symptom formation – it must be acknowledged that many people die happily frustrated! However, it is also true that an ounce of prevention is worth a pound of cure. There are many indications that sex is a problem concerning which uncertain feelings may provoke anxiety and guilt. The soaring sales which greet a book when the title has been altered to make it more suggestive constitute a case in point, for example, the change of a book entitled *The Fleece of Gold* to *The Quest for a Blond Mistress*; *The Case of Mr Crump* to *The Tyranny of Sex*. Or again one might consider the covers of many of the paper-bound novels which swarm in the drug-stores, groceries, restaurants, railroad stations, and book-stores in the United States today. It is true that the covers rarely have anything to do with the contents; often, however, they are sold on the basis of the covers alone. It has been said by a British philosopher that nine-tenths of the appeal of pornographic (obscene) literature is due to sex repression. If one were interested in advancing further points in support of this argument, one might note the names of magazines on the newstands in America today – *Male, Stag, Confidential, Tab, Bold, Frolic, Playboy, Whisper, Shock, Rave, Nite, Anything Goes, Bare, After Hours, Uncensored.* One has only to consider the differences in sexual *mores* between what is preached and what is practised (Kinsey) to make the thoroughly obvious point that sex is a matter about which our culture is hypersensitive. In such a setting, then, advertising promotion, whether for cars, soap, or vitamin pills, accentuates and exploits a situation of uncertain and repressed sexuality. Present-day advertising surrounding hypnosis is no exception.

'Are you lonely?' 'Do you want to gain the love and affection of the opposite sex – even *without* their knowledge?' 'Are you worried about sexual matters?' 'Do you realize that once in a trance your subject will do as you command and will obey your *every* wish?' (Italics *not* the author's.) The picture of a semi-nude female accompanying advertisements of this kind leaves little doubt as to what the wish may be. As a lure to learning hypnosis, one is promised, provided of course one buys a rather expensive book on how to hypnotize, twenty-four 'revealing' photographs. It is not made clear just what the photographs are 'revealing'. It is also interesting to note that the advertising concerning hypnosis gives the impression that the hypnotist is always a male and the subject always a solitary, well-shaped, good-looking, young, white girl in a flimsy negligée!

PERSONALITY

In the American culture and perhaps in other cultures the 'extravert' is the model of success. He is generally thought of as the happy-go-lucky, cigar-smoking, back-slapping, feet-on-the-desk, life-of-the-party individual. Outgoingness is the desired norm. A quiet, retiring person is looked upon with some suspicion as to whether he thinks the right thoughts or even has the right politics.

Want to – 'develop a strong powerful personality'? Want to – 'avoid being beset by personal mental problems'? Want to –

177

'steer clear of being anxious'? Want to – 'avoid being worried by domestic problems, mental obsessions, sleeplessness, or *any condition*'? If you wish to, it is all possible because a new 'magnetic personality' can be acquired through the study of hypnosis. Your old self is bound to change and you will be the 'centre of attraction'. Should a new personality not emerge, your money is cheerfully refunded, for results are guaranteed – so the advertising reads.

MIND-READING

Scientific experiments have attempted to find out whether mind-reading or mental telepathy is improved in the hypnotic state. No differences were found between the telepathic (mind-reading) ability of hypnotized and of non-hypnotized individuals.

Such a finding has not, however, impeded in the least those who are looking for the strange and mysterious in hypnosis. In point of fact, current popular magazines are not so much interested in *whether* mind-reading occurs (they assume that it does) as in *how* it occurs. This they generally answer by saying that the individual has two minds – the objective and the subjective. Mind-reading and hypnosis are said to be characteristic of the latter. The would-be demonstrator of mind-reading is told that the most suitable individuals for his experiments are 'females whose organizations are healthy'. What this means is not clear. It is true that a subject in hypnosis will describe in detail strange far-away places, make predictions of the future, and report on events which are occurring thousands of miles away. This all seems astonishing and wonderful, the audience marvels, but no one bothers to check on whether or not the statements made are true. Were such a check to be made, hypnosis would be robbed of this mysterious aspect which is so often exploited by charlatans.

A rather clever and convincing appearance of clairvoyance may result from crystal gazing. By getting the subject to stare at a crystal, a hypnotic state may be induced. Thereupon a post-hypnotic suggestion is given to the effect that the subject will go home, will look up a certain date in an old diary (after this has been ascertained to exist), and will believe that it had been predicted what the subject would read there. Amnesia is then suggested for the fact that there was any lapse in consciousness. As a result of this procedure, the subject (victim) is unaware of having been hypnotized, goes home, reads the diary, and is greatly impressed by this supposed display of clairvoyance. While the event described above actually took place, occurrences of this kind seem to be relatively rare.

In many cases what is interpreted as mind-reading is actually muscle-reading. For example, the supposed mind-reader may ask his subject to think of a corner of the room. By touching the subject's wrist the mind-reader will be able to detect the presence of very slight (minimal) muscular cues which will indicate to him the particular corner of the room being thought of. While this trick is generally done with the subject in a hypnotic state, neither hypnosis nor mind-reading is in any way involved.

More serious in implication are the letters received by government agencies, senators, and press, in which people complain of someone far off, generally in an enemy country, reading and controlling as well as torturing their minds by the use of hypnosis. Such complaints may be indicative of the presence of a serious mental illness characterized by fairly well-systematized beliefs. To a person unacquainted with the nature of this disturbance, the avowals of persecution, because of their systematized nature, are quite convincing. An editorial writer in a prominent American newspaper mentioned receiving just such a letter. Judging from his column, he was at first convinced of its validity, then hesitant. He concluded as follows: 'But after pondering the communications, and interviewing the author, all that I can say is the whole thing is above my head.' The net effect of the appearance of such a statement and the nature of the conclusion reached amount to support of already widespread misinformation about hypnosis.

There is no evidence that hypnosis favours mind-reading (assuming there is such a thing) in any way.

179

In public performances hypnosis may not actually be used even though the act is advertised and referred to as a 'hypnotic act' or as 'hilarious hypnosis'. The procedure when performing in a theatre is somewhat as follows: the 'hypnotist' obtains six or seven volunteers from the audience and – here the crux of the act is involved – obtains their cooperation in 'fooling the audience'. This is usually done by whispering instructions to the volunteers, which the audience, unable to hear, thinks is part of inducing hypnosis. If the stage hypnotist performs the proper antics, the audience is guaranteed to 'howl and roar' (and probably resolve never to be subjects for hypnosis). Certainly the writer has no objection to seeing people enjoy themselves. Nevertheless, he is concerned with *what* they are laughing at and its possible consequences.

Before describing some of the antics which cause such uproariousness in the audience a pertinent question should first be answered. Supposing the stage hypnotist encounters an uncooperative volunteer, one who will not help spoof the audience – what then? Here the pamphlet tells exactly what to do with such a 'refractory' individual.

Standing directly in front of the subject, push his head way back and then place the fingers of your hands on the side of the neck just below the ears a bit towards the throat. In such a position your fingers will be directly over the large veins of the neck (one on each side). You can locate these easily as they pulsate and throb beneath your fingers. Having so placed your fingers directly over these veins, press in gently but firmly upon them, at the same time requesting the man to breathe deeply (even if he doesn't wish to comply, he will be largely compelled to breathe deeply in order to get air in such a position, with his head so bent back). Maintain pressure upon the veins of his throat for a few moments, carefully watching your subject. You will find that he will suddenly go limp. Catch this moment and shout loudly 'sleep!' and let him slump down unconscious in his chair. . . . After that demonstration you will find that the subject will be most docile and willing to follow whatever whispered instructions you care to give. It also serves to impress the other subjects on the stage to the end that they had better cooperate along with you – or else.

A footnote further on tells you not to press too hard or too long! It is hoped that anyone foolish enough to follow these instructions will at least read the footnote, or he will have a dead subject on his hands as a result of cerebral anoxia (oxygen deprivation of the brain). Such a procedure for the rapid induction of hypnosis, while infrequently employed, may legitimately be used – but certainly not on the stage, where it is highly hazardous.

Sometimes in place of this pseudo demonstration of hypnosis, real hypnosis is utilized by employing post-hypnotic suggestion. Giving a post-hypnotic signal often adds to the idea of mystery surrounding hypnosis, for its operation unless understood furthers the suspicion of many that there is something 'eerie' in hypnosis. In a procedure which employs a post-hypnotic signal given from the stage, the very call for volunteers may constitute the signal for the resurgence of the hypnotic state. The writer has made use of the post-hypnotic signal in just such a way. Coming into a class (graduate psychology students), the writer stated that today he was going to consider hypnotherapy. A student in the back of the room was heard to whisper quite audibly, 'I'll bet he can't hypnotize me'. The writer, who could not help but hear the remark, said that inasmuch as little is known about the characteristics of those who are susceptible to hypnosis the individual who had made this comment might just as well be the subject. When this person came to the front of the class, the experimenter looked intently at him, clapped his hands, and in a loud tone said 'Be rigid'. Much to the amazement of the rest of the class, the individual was found to be in a deep hypnotic state as revealed by various tests of hypnosis. It was later explained to the class, by way of warning, that to the casual observer a mystical aspect of hypnosis often seems to be present. This is especially true, and is deliberately sought after on the stage. What had happened, the class was told, was the following: the hypnotic subject, the one who had whispered loudly, had visited the writer the day before the demonstration, and the writer had learned that he had been hypnotized previously and was deeply susceptible. This person had then been hypnotized and given the post-hypnotic suggestion that at the appropriate

181

signal (when the writer mentioned that today he was going to consider hypnotherapy), he was to say in an audible whisper that he could not be hypnotized and that when the writer clapped his hands and said, 'Be rigid', he would enter a deep hypnotic state. The hypnotist might just as easily and effectively have indicated that the post-hypnotic signal was to be the scratching of his head or the words 'slippery slug'. Thus the appearance of many seemingly peculiar phenomena results simply from post-hypnotic suggestion. Hypnotizing by means of a telephone, telegram, letter, playing-card, cat, or a glass of water can mysteriously occur, but represents nothing more than the action of a post-hypnotic suggestion.

In effect, then, the stage hypnotist may (1) simulate hypnosis, (2) bring his own subjects and have them react to a post-hypnotic signal, (3) advertise for subjects beforehand and have them respond to a post-hypnotic suggestion (usually the signal is the asking for volunteers);* or in rare cases (4) the stage hypnotist may attempt genuine hypnosis. However, having his eye on contract renewals or on an extended stay, the stage hypnotist rarely takes chances. The net result of the use of the first three methods, apart from emphasizing the uncanny, is to give the public the incorrect idea that one short session is all that is needed for inducing hypnosis. This works to the disadvantage of the professional hypnotherapist or experimentalist.

The original question concerned what the stage hypnotist did that was so funny to the audience – the answer is many things (the more brash the behaviour shown the more likely is the presence of actual rather than simulated hypnosis). Stage volunteers for hypnosis have been told that they are well-known popular singers and have sung, often in an obnoxious monotone, before a large audience. The author was acquainted with a rather quiet, self-conscious individual who volunteered (although the very act of volunteering could make one question

* The following is the sort of advertisement through which volunteers . are obtained :

'Wanted – Young men and women who have been, or who are willing to be, hypnotized. State age, sex, etc. Replies strictly confidential. Box 58 Province'.

how quiet and self-conscious he was), and was told that he was a well-known popular singer. Upon being told this, he sang in front of a large audience numbering in the hundreds – and sang horribly. A volunteer may be told that an old broom is a beautiful actress to whom he is to make love, or conversely he may be told that a good-looking girl making advances to him is an ugly old hag and that he will repulse her – all of which he does, much to the vast amusement of the audience. Or again a comedy routine may be centred about the inability (real or faked) to unclasp one's hands when requested to do so. A person in hypnosis on the stage may be told that he is now a little child and that he 'will laugh and play as if he were', then that he is a very old person – 'the transformation from youth to old age is very funny', or that he is 'deaf', 'blind', 'lame', 'ill', or 'very sad'. If the audience at the stage show or at the party is responsive and if one wishes to amuse them further, it is suggested that one tell the volunteer that he 'has fallen into the river' or that he is 'being chased by a wild animal' (a favourite technique, it appears). As a grand finale, it is suggested that the hypnotist make the old men among the volunteers do a 'cake walk'. These things are absolutely guaranteed to induce 'shriek after shriek of laughter'. Stage and parlour tricks like these are without number and are unfortunate not only because of the attitudes towards hypnosis which they create, but also because they are potentially dangerous (ch. XI) to the unwitting volunteers.

The alleged demonstration of reincarnation by regression in hypnosis is a sad commentary on how easily people may be taken in. One of the best 'non-fiction' sellers on the American scene was a book which purported to prove reincarnation through hypnosis. This book, which has been described as producing a 'hypnotic explosion' and from which a film has been made, may be described as a hunk of junk. What is done in practice is to bring the person back in years until he is zero and still further back, and then – and then – a reincarnated spirit of an individual living in a previous century is said to manifest itself. Instances of this are conveniently located in the far past or when in the near present have so many logical and experimental holes in them that they are best described as not even naïve! Telling a hypnotized subject that he is someone else who lived before in a different century, in a different land, and that he will be able to answer all questions will often result in his believing this and taking the proper role (ch. XIV). A mixture of specific instructions given by the hypnotist, lack of information about the background of the hypnotized subject, *naïveté,* peppered with hypnosis, will give the *appearance* of reincarnation. It might be mentioned that progression into the future has also been attempted with no difficulty whatsoever encountered in having the hypnotized subject describe what he will be doing in the future. It seems safe and far removed from confirmation to describe events that may happen in two hundred years (or in regression two hundred years ago), but woe betide the individual who attempts to predict what will happen in a year or a week from today, for then validation of the prediction is possible. To return to the present emphasis, which is on regression rather than progression into the future, it may be noted that regression in one lifetime is difficult enough to substantiate without attempting to return to different and many lifetimes. The logical culmination of this backward trend may be to reproduce monkey sounds – in which case poor biology and poor psychology would be involved. The question why people who 'don't know what to do with themselves on a rainy afternoon' want to 'outlive the sun and the stars' by believing in reincarnation is an interesting question, but not one that it is feasible to explore in this book. The belief that hypnosis by regression is able to accomplish many impossible things is also unfortunate, as is illustrated by the case of the old woman who had been blind forty years (p. 102).

Apart from unfortunate beliefs about hypnosis and possible dangers that may be involved in such demonstrations, other attitudes, as seen in the following, may also be engendered. 'Tie up your handkerchief and tell your subject that it is his little son, he will take care of it with the fondest attention. Tell him it cries and he will attempt to hush it to sleep. Suggest that he is holding a coloured baby, and he will throw it down in disgust.' A narrow and bigoted attitude in addition to charlatanism is revealed.

The financial aspect looms large as an important motivating factor for all kinds of behaviour. While it is true that the *nouveau riche* may be looked upon with a certain disquietude, nevertheless much can be overlooked or forgiven when money is present. A kleptomaniac (a person who has an irresistible impulse to steal) is sometimes humorously defined as a rich man's son who robs, or a person with money who commits suicide meets 'accidental death' and so on. Such expressions as 'What's in it for me?', 'Money talks', 'The almighty dollar', 'A penny saved is a penny earned', or 'It takes money to make money' are not just accidental expressions. This financial aspect is also to be seen in teaching, demonstrating, and writing about hypnosis.

In a recent little pamphlet on hypnosis a section is entitled 'How to Make Money out of Hypnosis'. In it are a lot of 'useful hints' about how much to charge. An evening's entertainment is said to be worth $25 to $50, teaching the art of hypnosis $5 for each method taught or a total of $50, correspondence courses are variously priced depending upon how much the traffic will bear, and so on. Higher rates may be charged if people believe you are 'really a Wonderful Person'. This little book then goes on, unfortunately, to relate that 'the largest sums are to be made by cures', 'by breaking bad habits', and by 'making good children out of bad ones', as well as by curing various and sundry other maladies. One is told in a sanctimonious tone that if one proceeds correctly in such therapeutic work, one may be called 'Blessed'. In reading this material one wonders rather idly why it is that if hypnosis and hypnotic demonstrations are such gold-mines the authors of this little pamphlet bother to write such a book which sells for a relatively modest sum.

Mail courses, demonstrations, pamphlets, 'schools' of hypnosis – any of these are said to offer huge financial returns and to require little in the way of preparation. Though the price range varies from 25c. to $150, the material offered in all these advertisements is essentially quite similar. The main difference seems to lie in the facts that 'schools' use live subjects, and the more expensive correspondence courses use a better brand of paper. For purposes of prestige, these schools are sometimes referred to as institutes or by the name of a minor religious sect.

At one such 'school' in the heart of a large eastern city in the United States, the writer applied in person. He inquired as to what was involved in enrolling. It seemed that the pre-requisite for this course in hypnosis was the possession of $35. For this sum a complete course in hypnosis (six lessons) would be given. Furthermore, it would include a 'very beautiful' 14 × 17 inch certificate of graduation. The 'school' guaranteed results (the kind was not specified). On asking the 'registrar' whether the person in charge of the course was qualified, the writer was told in no uncertain terms that the 'professor' possessed plenty of experience – twenty years on the stage! As the writer expressed his regret at not being able to enrol and backed away, the cost of the course decreased and the size of the graduation certificate increased!

For those who do not wish to have face-to-face contact with individuals, as would be required in conducting classes, correspondence courses may represent a solution. Such correspondence courses emphasize in their advertising the fact that 'You do not have to attend classes. There is no costly tuition fee. The complete course delivered to your home or office is small.' There is a great market here, or so it is claimed, since house wives and salesmen are very eager for this kind of course. The cost, it is true, may still be in the neighbourhood of one hundred dollars, but there are 'ironclad guarantees', and furthermore this is not just modern hypnosis but ultra-modern! Such correspondence courses have directors with honorary degrees and Vandyke beards. On passing an examination given by the 'school' or correspondence course (the passing mark appears to be completion of financial payments), a beautiful diploma, plus a plastic-sealed wallet-size miniature of the diploma, are sent, certifying the individual as a 'professional hypnotist'. These diplomas, the advertisement goes on to say, 'cannot be bought at any price'. Such courses are open to physicians, dentists, psychologists (so far so good) and – any serious student! The 'degree' given in such a course of study is the 'Hyp.D.'. This

'degree' refers to a Doctor of Hypnosis – although more appro-
priately from reading their literature it might better be called
Doctor of Hypocrisy! One institute (named after a famous
university but having nothing to do with it) advertises hypnosis
which will reveal the secrets of financial success, sexual har-
mony, will-power, magnetic personality, weight reduction, and
any other problems that may be thought of. Still another course
promised that on learning hypnosis (by this correspondence
course) the hypnotist could then 'eradicate' bedwetting, bad
dreams, fears, apprehensions, stealing, cheating, and lying.
These courses cost from $25 to $125 and consist of about a
dozen lessons. These lessons, the writer was informed, teach
how to : test for hypnotic subjects, induce hypnosis, conduct a
living-room party session, produce anaesthesia, produce catalepsy, direct the routine for a two-hour hypnotic stage show,
elicit telepathy, create publicity, and hypnotize people without
their knowledge.

Included with these advertisements for correspondence
courses were testimonials, mostly unsigned, describing the many
benefits attendant upon buying these courses. One is told in these
leaflets that the majority if not all subjects go under in one
minute, but that if one takes this course offered at a 'ridiculously
low price', it will take even less time! If the subject is being
hypnotized for the first time, the time period indicated is very
short. However, if the subject has been hypnotized before and
is responding to a post-hypnotic suggestion, then the time period
indicated is very long. The information which the writer received contained many other germs of wisdom: weak-willed persons cannot be hypnotized because they are too 'wishy-washy',
and many other such statements which at best confound confusion or are outright lies. If one does not take advantage of
such an opportunity, one is, so it is said, missing a rare experience and failure to purchase one of the home courses for the
learning of hypnosis clearly indicates that you 'just don't want
to improve your future'.

If, however, one's taste does not run to either conducting
classes or writing correspondence courses, one can then give
private or public entertainments of hypnosis at a handsome

profit. It may be mentioned in passing that the master of ceremonies for a hypnotist performing at a night-club had previously been pictured in the press in revealing women's clothes
and publicized as 'the World's Most Beautiful Man'. This is
mentioned and is of interest only in giving some idea of the
context in which hypnosis is seen and known to the public.

The author received a pamphlet about what every hypnotist
should know about publicity. This little pamphlet told him that
if he wished to obtain such publicity he must: make a trade-
mark of some aspect of his physical appearance, get at least one
thousand photographs of himself, have prepared news releases
(not over two hundred words in length), tie in with something
newsworthy, make use of any and all kinds of conventions (if
it should be an appliance convention, tell them that hypnosis
also makes use of appliances; if a home convention, tell them
that hypnosis may be done in the home!), be interviewed by disc
jockeys, use free guest spots on television, use the hypnotized-
beautiful-model-in-silk-pyjamas-in-a-store-window routine (the
girl, one is told, does not have to be a model, but she should
always be referred to as one), have nerve, and finally subscribe
to a press-cutting service.

One other avenue of profitable business exists. One may sell
at a handsome price hypnodiscs, hypnoscopes, pocket sized
metronomes, hypnotic brow-lights, hypnocoins, and power
keys, all devices it is said that help in inducing hypnosis. These
apparatuses which are to be fixated upon consist of elaborate
flashing lights, whirling spirals, and the like. If one is not 'de-
lighted' with such tools of hypnosis, the money is cheerfully
refunded. In addition to many dubious articles, books which
may be serious or farcical are sold. In one advertisement the
writer saw publicized serious books alongside encyclopaedias
of stage hypnosis and books on how to recognize faces.

Confusion as well as misinformation abound. In reply to
advertisements for hypnosis taken from cheap pulp magazines,
the author found that one group had ceased to function, a
second group for reasons unknown to the author sent books
proving the existence of a dog heaven, and a third organization

was never heard from. Furthermore, it was found that so-called scientific journals had articles on serious bona-fide problems in hypnosis alongside completely irrelevant and meaningless ones.

Finally, a sign of the times, there is a 'get hypnotized' booth at the Svengali Club at a large amusement resort on the east coast of the United States.

THE FUTURE

Misuse of hypnosis and its unfortunate by-products are only too obvious. There are, however, some optimistic signs. In England laws have made it more difficult for the stage hypnotist to 'entertain'. In the United States the Society for Clinical and Experimental Hypnosis is opposed to the use of hypnosis for amusement purposes. This group is not only trying to educate the public about hypnosis, but is at the same time attempting to secure legislation prohibiting the employment of hypnosis for entertainment purposes (ch. XIII). Pending the time when such laws are obtained its members are alert for the possibility that hypnosis may be misused.

It would seem that in public and private demonstrations of hypnosis there are many factors: hypocrisy, hysterics, horror, heterosexuality, hooey, hogwash – everything but hypnosis. The very individuals, often psychologists and medical men, who deride public belief in fads which emphasize the supernatural, often in the form of reincarnation or some other pseudo-scientific belief, actually contribute to these misguided beliefs. For if we knew more about the nature of hypnosis, the study of which these individuals generally oppose, such obvious frauds could not continue.

189

Chapter XIII

ET CETERA

'ANIMAL HYPNOSIS'

THE writer first started experimenting on 'animal hypnosis' when experiments in human hypnosis were banned (ch. II). Inasmuch as animals have no alumni, it was considered permissible to investigate this area.

Why is the term 'animal hypnosis' usually written in quotation marks or why is it sometimes referred to as 'so-called animal hypnosis'? Both usages reflect our ignorance of the phenomenon. A question often asked is why we say 'animal hypnosis' when the word 'hypnosis' is meaningful only when applied to humans, and the word 'animal' as used here has nothing to do with human beings. If this is confusing – and it is – consider the concept 'animal magnetism' which has nothing to do with animals! Such loose and confusing terms tend to muddy the issue, and as a result animal and human hypnosis are often equated. Doing this involves a serious error, for the behaviour of the most complicated animals is much simpler and easier to understand than that of the simplest of men. This is not to deny that there are certain similarities in comparing animal and human hypnosis, but there are also vast important and definite differences. Repetition of 'hypnotic' induction, for example, has an opposite effect on animals (decreases susceptibility) and on human beings (increases susceptibility). One might say that the thug lurking behind a building and waiting for his intended victim has some points of similarity with the octopus lurking behind a rock and waiting for its intended victim. Here, however, the similarity ends and the differences begin, for an octopus may 'lurk' behind a transparent piece of glass, but few if any burglars would expose themselves to this extent. As one continues to analyse the thug and the octopus, it becomes clear that the whole atmosphere surrounding them differs. In describing animals we generally do not talk of the attitude of the amoeba, the aspirations of the ass, the plans of the pig, the nationality of the nannygoat, or the religion of the rat, but in man we do. Science, it is true, is interested in similarity, but it is also of necessity interested in differences – a simple point, yet one that is often ignored. The use of the term animal hypnosis may be said to arise from consideration of similarities alone.

What kind of animals are subject to animal hypnosis and what are its characteristics? Very many kinds of animals are susceptible and, as might be expected, the results obtained depend upon whether one is working with a relatively simple animal like the amoeba or a more complicated one like the chimpanzee. One feature of animal hypnosis, however, which seems to be common to many kinds of animals throughout the evolutionary scale is loss of the ability to move. Such immobility when elicited may last anywhere from fifteen seconds to thirty minutes. The procedure which appears to elicit this type of response (immobility) is restriction of activity. Apart from fairly general agreement about the loss of motor ability in all kinds of animals, everything else is disputed, including respiration rate, heart rate, anaesthesia, and other characteristics. Such a confused state is probably due to the fact that experiments have not only had different kinds and levels of animals as subjects in their investigations but have also employed different techniques of inducing so-called animal hypnosis.

How is animal hypnosis induced? It used to be thought, and popularly still is, that this was accomplished by drawing a chalk line in front of a chicken, by staring into the eyes of a bird, or by breathing on the head of a horse. Why these things were thought to be relevant for inducing animal hypnosis is not clear. However, in order to do these things the animal must first be held firmly, and thus restriction of activity will, willy-nilly, be present. It can only be said of the early techniques mentioned above that there was a waste of chalk, stare, and air. In selecting an adequate technique for inducing animal hypnosis, feasibility is important. The possibility of physical restriction with the cockroach is obvious, straightforward, and direct, for the cockroach may be inverted and held still with impunity, but this cannot be done with a lion or a horse. In addition to restriction, the presence of a sudden and generally strong stimulus often seems to be effective in producing this immobility which is sometimes referred to as 'freezing' behaviour in certain animals. Individual differences even in animals cannot be ignored. When a monotonous stimulus was utilized in addition to restriction on three pigs, they reacted to the same stimulus, stroking the underbelly, in radically different ways even though they had the same mother, were born at the same time, were of the same sex, and were the same weight. One appeared to become blissfully unaware of her environment and remained motionless; a second became angry, very active, and roared her disapproval; while the third was indifferent and bored. It would thus appear that an unwarranted degree of sameness cannot be assumed at the animal level any more than at the human level. One rat, chicken, or pig is not identical with another rat, chicken, or pig. While it is certainly not the writer's contention that life among the infra-humans is in any way as complex as that among humans; nevertheless, it is more complex than may at first be assumed.

Theories of animal hypnosis vary widely and few tend to agree with one another. Some theories claim to explain all of the evidence, while some more modestly claim to explain only part of it. Among the various theories some emphasize the role of fear, some the resemblance to human hypnosis, and some the question of death-feigning. The last-mentioned theory enjoys popular and widespread belief and deserves some comment, even though, as with most theories of animal hypnosis, it lacks proof. Death-feigning assumes that an animal in danger becomes immobile by falling into a hypnotic state resembling death and by so doing escapes the attention of its would-be foe, thus saving its life. In this way the concept of death-feigning is said to have survival value. Such a theory raises many questions. Does the animal in the death feint actually look dead? Do all or only some animals possess this ability? If only some, why? Does it occur only when an animal needs protection, or does it also occur when flight is indicated? Does an immobile animal recover ability as soon as its erstwhile foe has departed? Such questions as the above make one wonder whether or not this particular theory of death-feigning does possess biological survival value. Probably, like animal camouflage, it has some survival value, but is far from perfect. Pessimism about ever formulating a theory of animal hypnosis is not so much indicated as is the need for more precise definition of just what animal hypnosis is, and the obtaining of more data from various kinds and levels of animals. Until such time as we have such data, it is doubtful that any widely acceptable theory of 'animal hypnosis' can be formulated.

Despite advances (small though they be) that have added to our scientific knowledge of animal hypnosis, quack advertising on this problem prefers to keep abreast of the information available a hundred years ago. One reads that only some individuals can hypnotize both animals and human beings, some just animals, and so on. One may also be told that a chicken can be hypnotized by drawing a chalk line in front of it, a pigeon by placing a small piece of white putty at the end of its beak, and a vicious horse by grabbing its nose firmly, drawing its head down and blowing 'strong and steadily into its ear for about five minutes'. (Just blowing for five minutes is itself a difficult feat.)

LEGISLATION

The situation confronting one in this area is chaotic. The majority of American states lack legislation of any kind regarding the control of hypnosis. Where legal control is present, the laws are either ambiguous or weak. The necessity of laws to protect the public as well as the psychologist is obvious. In the extreme one might argue that if crimes can be committed in and by hypnosis, certainly there is reason for legislation.

There are essentially two kinds of legislative bills, those to certify and those to license. The former is said to be permissive and defines who is eligible to use hypnosis. The latter is said to be restrictive and, by implication if not directly, says who cannot use hypnosis. Both types of bills have penalties attached to them, although generally those associated with licensing are

193

more severe. Both types of bills may overlap and are not always easy to differentiate. In the State of Washington, U.S.A., a certification bill for psychologists has been in force for some years. Among the various points made by the framers of this bill is that they may refuse to grant a certificate if there is proof that the individual requesting certification has acted unethically. Such an unethical act may be 'the employment of psychological techniques for entertainment or for other purposes not consistent with the development of psychology as a science'. Hypnosis may conceivably take advantage of this clause. However, implementation of this aspect of the law to protect hypnosis from being an entertainment medium is sharply limited. Few if any professional entertainers are interested in, let alone have the required background for, obtaining certification. Consequently they would not come under this section of the law. While the law itself may be a step in the right direction, it is a short one and it may constitute a difference that makes no difference as regards the practice of hypnosis. The situation in about a dozen states in the United States is similar to that described for Washington. In short, there has been no successful attempt to outlaw hypnosis completely as an entertainment medium, a procedure which has partially succeeded in England (in 1953 a law was passed banning demonstrations on persons under twenty-one years of age). In the United States certain other bills which take into account only the abuses of hypnosis have attempted to outlaw it entirely – a case of throwing out the baby with the bath water.

The attitude of the Society for Clinical and Experimental Hypnosis, characteristic of the serious workers in this field, is simply that hypnosis should no more be a subject for entertainment than should appendicitis, a decayed tooth, or cancer. The Society's attitude with regard to legislation is important in that one could legitimately assume that in this group would be found those who are most concerned with problems of control and who have given it most thought. As a first step, the Society polled its own members to find out what areas of agreement there were within the group. On the basis of this poll, it was found that there was agreement on the need for: prohibiting

194

the use of hypnosis for entertainment, obtaining certification rather than licensing, establishing a code of ethics, and finally, as might be expected, investigating the problem further. Should there be legislation, they are desirous that it be well-conceived and thought-out, and not thrown out on a technicality. For should a poorly conceived hypnotic bill fail, its precedent-setting role might well constitute an obstacle in the future to hypnotic control bills which are both good and legally sound. It is, however, rather difficult to impress a legislature or to seek cooperation from other groups if there are little more than a few hundred people behind a movement.

In attempting to obtain the necessary laws prohibiting the use of hypnosis as an entertainment medium, hypnosis may be thought of in its two phases – experimental and clinical. Legislation protecting the therapeutic or clinical aspect of hypnosis may have to be found indirectly in the current medical definition of therapeutic practice. The research aspect of hypnosis may find protection in the present attempt to enact legislation prohibiting the use of hypnosis for entertainment purposes.

An important point involved in legislation for control of hypnosis is to whom the practice of hypnosis should be restricted. While there is some fighting among professional groups (doctors, psychiatrists, psychologists, dentists) as to who among them is qualified by training to use hypnosis (clinical rather than experimental), they tend to close ranks when it comes to the consideration of whether lay hypnotists should be allowed to employ hypnosis. They would legislate in such a way that lay hypnotists could no longer operate – but should they? It might be argued that a lay group of hypnotists could function beneficially and be utilized to advantage by clinicians. It might also be argued that it is this kind of group with its large membership which may have the time and energy to devote to public education, for their aims are very similar to the professional aims that have been described elsewhere (p. 34). On the negative side is the unfortunate fact that most, though not all, of the misusers of hypnosis, those that promise the impossible, are to be found in this group. It is in the lay group that we find 'the erstwhile carnival hustler turned doctor'. Many but not all of the lay hypnotist groups are in the business of hypnosis for one reason only – financial returns. In the semi-scientific journals of well-meaning lay groups are articles with poor experimental design and even poorer logic. Also to be found are advertisements in the poorest of taste. But the horrible thought occurs to one that possibly they just cannot afford to be too scientific and still maintain their circulation.

Spokesmen for the lay groups oppose those who would legislate them out of existence at the same time as they seek to eradicate the charlatans within their own ranks. They point out, quite correctly, that the possession of a degree does not necessarily equip one to decide about human behaviour, although by the same logic neither does possession of no degree.

It would be the author's recommendation that any professionally qualified individual who has met certain minimum standards set up by a professionally interested group be allowed to utilize hypnosis in his own specialty. In addition he would limit (not abolish) the lay use of hypnosis to therapy supervised by a professionally qualified clinician. Use of hypnosis for entertainment even in 'good taste' would be prohibited.

INSURANCE

A question related to legislation concerning hypnosis is that of 'blackmail' insurance. Related because the lack of adequate laws concerning the control of hypnosis increases the probability of the charge of malpractice. One professional organization in its insurance policy specifically excludes the practice of hypnosis from coverage. In the attempt to clarify this rather murky and ambiguous situation, many procedures are resorted to. Some psychologists working with hypnosis require a release from the parents of their subject, some refuse to work with female subjects in individual experiments, while others always have a third person present regardless of whether the work is experimental or clinical. It has already been indicated how such procedures may foster attitudes unfavourable to understanding and to research in hypnosis. For such procedures suggest that there is something in hypnosis that is potentially harmful or tend to reduce the number of possible subjects in experiments.

While medical practitioners are covered by malpractice insurance, this was not the case with non-medical researchers until recently. Some non-medical researchers believe, and this is erroneous, that personal liability insurance protects them against malpractice charges in much the same fashion that they would be covered if a visitor in their house injured himself by falling down the stairs. Others seem to hold, but again it is a vain hope, that the obtaining of a release from the subject or from the subject's parents (if he is under twenty-one years of age) protects them from a lawsuit. Happily malpractice insurance has been available since 1955 to psychologists, and this protects them 'against *any* claim for alleged malpractice, error, or mistake in the rendering or failure to render professional services'. When the writer inquired whether or not this covered the use of hypnosis, the answer was in the affirmative.

TRAINING

Doctors, dentists, clinicians, or research psychologists may be impressed by the application of hypnosis both experimental and therapeutic, but where, they may ask, could a properly qualified individual obtain the necessary training in hypnosis. While admittedly the provision for such training is sparse, it does exist. Nowadays work of value to hypnosis is being done by medically, dentally, and psychologically trained individuals.* Consequently what competent training is to be found is in these areas. In the United States, seminars some two to four days in length have been offered with qualified instructors. These individuals possess a professional degree, are experienced in the applied use of hypnosis, are aware of its research possibilities,

* In 1958 the American Medical Association recognized the legitimate use of hypnosis and suggested that 'teaching related to hypnosis be under responsible medical or dental direction'. Whether an individual is competent to employ hypnosis should be a question of examination (as proposed by the Society for Clinical and Experimental Hypnosis), and not one of arbitrary fiat. The writer, as Chairman of the S.C.E.H. Committee on Ethics, was not convinced that misuses were the domain of, or foreign to, any one profession. Cooperation rather than supervision seems to be indicated.

and are conversant with its theoretical aspects. Such courses have a fee of from $50 to $100, are restricted to those who already possess a professional degree, and include lectures, demonstrations, and actual experience in hypnotic induction. Unfortunately, such seminars, because of shortage of time, often stress techniques of induction. This can be, and often is, an error. For it is certainly equally important to know what can and what cannot be accomplished once the induction of hypnosis has been successful. One should, in addition, also know something about the general subject-matter of hypnosis. The importance of successful experience in hypnotic induction should not, however, be minimized. A beginner may be discouraged by encountering, as is very possible, failures in his first four or five subjects. As a consequence of this, the would-be hypnotist, in addition to feeling slightly foolish, may turn against hypnosis. It is an unfortunate truism that many individuals react defensively to that which they know little about or in which they consistently fail. Supervised work presenting both successful and unsuccessful cases to the beginner would avoid this particular pitfall. In short, a course should present both the advantages and the limitations of hypnosis.

Unfortunately, there is still a dearth of training facilities at the present time in the United States, even in dentistry in which that country is reputed to be advanced. A realistic concrete though rather sad illustration will serve as an example of this situation. A qualified professional man, A, wishing to be instructed about the uses of hypnosis, wrote to B (the writer), who referred him in good faith to C who had a similar professional background to A and furthermore was president of a professional society utilizing hypnosis. C in turn, however, referred him to D, an official of the Society for Clinical and Experimental Hypnosis, who in turn referred him back to B – and thus the slightly unfortunate circle was completed.

There are professional societies of dentists with their own journals for individuals who are already dentists who may desire some form of postgraduate training. While there are such groups as the American Society for the Advancement of Hypnodontics, the American Society for Psychosomatic Dentistry as well as local groups, they lack adequate facilities for instruction, and are all located in a few large cities. Such groups were organized around the year 1948, and there have been moves to amalgamate the various groups in order that the body so formed may be more effective. The ethical code of these societies is that of the American Dental Association, and its aims are to discourage the use of hypnosis for entertainment, to discourage its use by the unqualified, and to encourage those legitimately concerned with the use of hypnosis in dentistry. Such groups have lists of qualified instructors who have been certified by the various groups as postgraduate teachers. Such certification usually involves the possession of an appropriate professional degree, belonging to a recognized professional society, and having the requisite experience. At the present time there are some fifty of these instructors who have trained sometimes formally, sometimes informally, some hundreds of dentists.

Until lately there has been only an apprentice-like type of training available. Recently, however, at an eastern American university there has been established a course on hypnosis for dentists. It consists of three successive units, each unit requiring three hours a week for fourteen weeks, and is taught by professionally experienced individuals. The first unit of this course consists of history, phenomena, induction, and contemporary hypnotic literature. The second unit deals with the physiology of emotions, conflict, personality, indicators and contraindicators of hypnosis, amnesia, and self-hypnosis. The final unit comprises a practicum, three or four dentists with one instructor, in which case-material is dealt with. The only adverse comment that the author would have for this welcome innovation is that it seems over-ambitious for the period allotted. But time alone will confirm or rectify this observation.

What of the person who does not yet possess the advanced degree; where does he get the necessary training? Again it must be emphasized that at present there is a limited number of outlets for such training. Courses that may be taken during graduate work in psychology concerned with the problems of hypnosis are relatively rare, and such courses are usually informal. There are also reading lists available which are concerned with such problems as history, induction, specialized application, and other areas. Should a person be interested in furthering his knowledge concerning the field of hypnosis, it is suggested that he write to the person in the field with whom he wishes to study, or get into contact with one of the societies referred to and inquire what would be the best procedure to follow. Often a graduate student is advised to take informal work in the area of hypnosis, and in this way, one hopes, the candidate will be exposed to the proper theoretical and practical experience required of one working in this area.

In other countries recognition of the positive values of hypnotherapy is often present, but outlets are again limited. In England there is the possibility of the medical group's providing such an outlet to ensure that students are 'properly grounded' in the study of hypnosis. This recommendation made by a committee of the British Medical Association has yet to materialize.

As long as proper outlets for legitimate training are not present, legislation will be hindered and quacks will flourish. If pending such a time the services of a properly qualified clinician who utilizes hypnotherapy are desired, the individual needing such service would be well advised to contact either the Society for Clinical and Experimental Hypnosis (United States) or the British Society of Medical Hypnotists (England).

SELF-HYPNOSIS

Many individuals have maintained, and with some reason, that all hypnosis is a function of self-hypnosis. They argue in effect that hypnosis induced by some other individual merely guides the subject along the channels indicated by himself, and that it is the hypnotized individual's expectations that are important in the manifestations obtained. They point to the results when hypnosis alone is induced without any kind of suggestion whatsoever. While such results have no outside suggestion this does not, they point out, preclude the presence of self-suggestion as an explanation of the results. On the other hand, other individuals have maintained, with equally good reason, that all self-hypnosis is a function of hypnosis proper, and that the expectations shown by the hypnotized subjects are derived from an outside source. Furthermore, they add that the kind of self-hypnosis usually encountered is induced by a post-hypnotic signal given to the subject by someone else. This 'outside-inside' argument is very much like the chicken and egg problem.

Self-hypnosis, or as it is often called autohypnosis, is said to have its major role in its therapeutic application. While it is often less expensive and more convenient for the patient to utilize self-hypnosis, it requires a deep hypnotic state, and thus it follows that only a small proportion of the general population can benefit by it. One technique for the induction of self-hypnosis is to give a post-hypnotic suggestion to the effect that the subject, on self-command, will go into a deep hypnotic state, but in every other respect will remain alert and in full contact with the environment. Autohypnosis may also be induced by slight modification of the procedure whereby others are hypnotized. This is often accomplished by having the subject start by staring at the tip of his nose. It is further indicated to the subject that in this state whatever suggestion (specified by the clinician in therapy cases) he gives himself will be effective. During World War II prisoners who possessed this ability were said to be better able to withstand long periods of cold by sending more warm blood to the affected areas. Hypnodontists have trained patients in self-hypnosis so that they themselves may control salivation as well as bring on anaesthesia (ch. X). Obstetricians may do likewise, inasmuch as labour may start suddenly. In general, however, the use of self-hypnosis in 'mental' or 'organic' problems is not considered wise, for the simple and compelling reason that the therapist generally wishes to keep in contact with his patient and to follow his progress or the lack of it. It is interesting to note that the experienced and professionally trained hypnotists (Preface) felt that this field especially had been oversold and its potential dangers unrecognized. The risk is that the person practising self-hypnosis may, through its use, submerge himself more and more into his own personal dream world to the exclusion of reality.

It may also be that the phenomenon of 'highway hypnosis' is a form of self-hypnosis brought on, over long distances, by the fixed staring at the road (vision), the unvaried hum of the engine (audition), and the, of necessity, constant posture (kinesthesis). While not too much is known about this subject, its potential danger is readily recognized. Any device or combination of devices which interferes with the deadly monotonous stimulation (visual, auditory, and kinesthetic) which the driver is subjected to could be of value. Such techniques would include stretching (when stopped), listening to the radio (with the possible exception of certain types of music), chewing gum, conversing, and so on.

Autosuggestion, self-suggestion, or Couéism ('Every day in every way I am getting better and better') is often difficult to differentiate in many cases from auto- or self-hypnosis. It is conceivable that one may branch over into the other, and that autohypnosis may often actually be autosuggestion and vice versa. It may be asked what kind of suggestion does autosuggestion involve. Self-deception and denial of reality (indirect suggestion) are sometimes seen 'n autosuggestion, but usually it is the direct type of suggestion related to hypnosis.

Some form of self-suggestion or self-hypnosis may account for the success of many present-day 'techniques for relaxing'. A movie star described her method of relaxing as follows: 'I close my eyes and picture an image of a black dot on a white background. . . . I see this black dot coming closer and closer, getting larger and larger, and as it completely takes over my thoughts I drift into a sound sleep. Along with this I breathe deeply and rhythmically. . . . It seemed I would never master it but I was persistent, and then one night I dropped off to sleep in a minute and ever since it has worked for me like a charm. . . . Once you master it you can sleep four minutes out of a five-minute break.'

MISCELLANEOUS FACTORS

BRAIN-WAVES

Electrical (electro) waves from the brain (encephalo) which are graphed (gram) are referred to as electroencephalograms, abbreviated to EEG. Certain types of brain-waves (there are many kinds), said to be characteristic of individuals, appear or disappear, depending upon the presence or absence of a specific stimulus such as audition or vision. The question arises as to whether or not such waves can be made to appear or disappear when the appropriate stimuli (visual or auditory) are suggested as present or absent in hypnosis without such stimuli actually being present or absent physically. In short, what is the effect of positive or negative hallucinations on electroencephalograms? All kinds of results have been reported. Probably the different kinds of results stem from the different depths of hypnosis obtained, from the different techniques of induction employed, and possibly from the different kinds of brain-waves originally present. When we consider that heart rate follows the course of hypnotic suggestion rather than physical reality, it would follow that brain-waves might also be similarly affected. But then again there is some evidence that brain-waves are responsive to suggestion even when the subject is not hypnotized. Induction of hypnosis without suggestion of any kind (and in the absence, it is assumed, of self-hypnosis) has no effect on brain-waves. The brain-waves during hypnosis are similar to those of the waking state, and can be differentiated from those of deep sleep – an important consideration for those who equate sleep and hypnosis (p. 209).

BRAINWASHING

The concept of brainwashing is a source of much confusion. It has been called various things: 'induced political psychosis', 'menticide', 'compartmentalized mental illness', 'conditioning', etc.; and as unfortunately might be expected, hypnosis. It has been described as having its beginning when a group of soldiers, captured by the enemy, instead of being shot as they were told to expect, were greeted as friends! While the term brainwashing is seen quite frequently in the press nowadays and conjures up all kinds of strange visions, it is most often used with reference to political ends. Thus it was said, and said by a person high up in the government of the United States, that the Supreme Court in ruling against Negro educational segregation must have been brainwashed by the left! This approach carried to an extreme may be seen in the recent statement that people in the West do not believe in reincarnation (living again in another body) because they have all been brainwashed! The statement that brainwashing is due to hypnosis or drugs reflects a sad confusion about drugs, hypnosis, and values.

In some countries brainwashing is looked upon with approval – but is now referred to as 'engineered consent'!

WARFARE

A possible function of hypnosis in war is to have a courier convey a verbal message whose nature is completely unknown to him. He is directed to a given person who rehypnotizes him and discovers the content of the message. The amnesia suggested in hypnosis disappears in response to a given code word. Should the courier be captured, he knows nothing of the message, and supposedly is unable to reveal any information under duress. The story, however, does not end here, for counter intelligence is prepared to meet such a situation by creating hallucinations about the courier's being at his destination and among compatriots, and then attempting to hypnotize him and obtain the enemy's message. Nor does the story end here, for to meet this in turn, the enemy's intelligence or counter intelligence may in hypnotizing the courier give him false information, arrange that he be captured, and be susceptible, and thus reveal to the enemy this false information. Then in turn the counter. . . . It may be said that very few are sufficiently susceptible to hypnosis to be suitable subjects for such an undertaking. While this is true, it may well be that the obtaining of even one such person may be worth the effort. It is relevant to note that an individual who was concerned with this type of work described it as 'unethical' and a 'dirty mess'.

CRIME

During a round-up of suspects an individual may be found who is susceptible to hypnosis by the disguise (sleep) method (p. 58). Such a person might conceivably be told, during hypnosis, to be on the lookout for information about the murder of a certain person. Such information, when and if obtained, might be elicited on the next round-up by rehypnotizing this individual again during sleep. The unwitting 'stool pigeon' believes in his own innocence, and this in all likelihood will be his best protection. Conceivable uses of hypnosis for criminal purposes would be: to secure false testimony, to obtain signatures, or to create a situation in which bodily attack might take place. In the extreme, as indicated in the annals of American crime, it is possible to have a murder committed. It would be regrettable either to have a guilty person employ hypnosis as a shield or to have an innocent person imprisoned because the law does not understand the possibilities inherent in hypnosis. As in warfare the obtaining of one such deeply susceptible person may be all that is needed.

SALESMANSHIP

Recently there appeared in a pulp magazine a request for aid from a salesman – because he was too successful! It seems that few could resist buying from him and that few employers could resist giving him a job. After he had sold 'tough' prospective clients items for which they actually had no use, they would realize what they had done and demand a refund. Since he seemed always to have worked for sterling, upright, and honest firms, the money was always refunded. His 'unfortunate' ability, he gravely informs us, was due to 'wild hypnosis'.

Such a situation will not appear quite as horrendous to individuals who are salesmen, for they in all likelihood would be more interested in learning this 'wild hypnosis' than in getting rid of it. It is recognized that certain individuals are more persuasive than others – why? The sale of, for example, an encyclopaedia is effected through a combination of factors, and may utilize the following: parental desire to educate his child (an obligation), flattery (the target of the sale had been specially selected – so it is said), feeling of indebtedness (the salesman often spends more than an hour in demonstrating the value of his goods), obtaining a 'real bargain' (a bookcase is included free), the personality of the salesman (an open-faced, frank, and 'sincere' young man), and so on. Next morning the victim wonders how and why he ever put his signature on the contract and what happened to his resistance. He then discovers that if he had really wanted the books, he could have obtained them at a lower price at the local bookstore. As a consequence of this finding, he tries to break the contract. When this is unsuccessful, as it generally is, he concludes in self-defence 'I must have been hypnotized'!

Wild hypnosis is nothing but the figment of a wild imagination. Successful salesmanship in no way relies on hypnosis.

Chapter XIV

THEORIES

A THEORY, according to definition, is a general principle which explains certain types of behaviour – in this case hypnosis. It may, furthermore, be said that theory should be inclusive of a mechanism which is intended to indicate just how the theory works. A theory, as defined above, is called upon to explain many different kinds of hypnotic phenomena. It may be called upon to explain the relaxation which is said to be produced to a greater extent in hypnosis than in the waking state, and at the same time it may be called upon to explain how hypnosis results from this greater relaxation. Or it may be called upon to try to explain or describe the relationship between patient and hypnotist. It is the contention of this writer that before we can elaborate a satisfactory theory of hypnosis, we must first answer a number of pertinent questions. Can we differentiate lighter stages of hypnosis from non-hypnotic persuasion? Have we a satisfactory scale of hypnotic depth? Is regression (return to an earlier phase of life) a true characteristic of hypnosis, is it fact or artifact? Do active and passive hypnosis require different theories? There are many many more questions that could be asked which concern attributes of hypnosis. These are all questions that require replies before an adequate theory of hypnosis can be formulated, but as yet no definite answers have been given. At present widely varying results are reported by individuals working with hypnosis, and as a consequence of this state of affairs there is uncertainty about its nature. Peculiar as it may seem, most theories of hypnosis assume a little bit of hypnosis to begin with, and then proceed to discuss how suggestion may magnify it. This is very much like talking of a woman being a little bit pregnant; it is meaningless not to deal with the initial response.

In evaluating the theories of hypnosis that are often described, certain precautions must be heeded. It should be realized that many of the theories that have been formulated have often depended upon the particular aspect of hypnosis that the theory-former has been interested in and working with. Thus, the physician who is concerned with the anaesthetic qualities of deep hypnosis would in all likelihood propose a theory different from that of the individual concerned with the lighter phases of hypnosis. The physician might be extremely critical of theories which stress role-playing and wonder just how these would attempt to explain the successful anaesthesia of surgical operations; whereas investigators using lighter phases of hypnosis would point to the high selectivity involved in the physicians' cases. Also important in the evaluation of a theory of hypnosis, or for that matter of any theory, is the year in which it was proposed, for the kinds of data available at the time play an important part in the development of any theory. In this respect one might say that an explanation of hypnosis in terms of animal magnetism (Mesmer) while erroneous in the light of present-day data, nevertheless brought the data of hypnosis into a workable frame of reference, and in this way actually made investigation possible. We must be careful about accepting theories which attempt to explain hypnosis as the working of the subconscious or unconscious mind. Such an interpretation is circular and not very meaningful, for these concepts themselves are not fully understood. Too often in theory formation we are in the questionable position of explaining 'X' by 'Y' when we are not sure what 'Y' is.

Five points should be kept in mind in considering any theory of hypnosis: the era in which it was suggested, the type of hypnosis referred to, the mechanism (if any) by which it operates, the fact that in this discussion the pros and cons of all theories are certainly not given, and finally that at the present time no theory is completely satisfactory.

Early theories included Mesmer's interpretation of mesmerism (hypnosis) in terms of animal magnetism. This belief held that a fluid (whose colour was even described) passed from the body of the hypnotist to that of the subject, and in this way produced its effects. Another early theory, if it may be so called, which enjoyed a brief existence held that the behaviour elicited in hypnosis was a direct function of the manual pressure exerted by the hypnotist on specific parts of the skull. Thus, for example, if manual pressure were exerted on the humour area (assuming there was one), then a joke might result and so on. Both of these early theories languished and died from lack of confirming data.

HYSTERIA

In the past it was thought, and to a certain extent still is, that only those who are emotionally unstable could be hypnotized. It was also believed that these people when they regained their emotional stability would no longer be hypnotizable. Such observations were based on only a few cases and failed to realize that when a patient was sick he tended to be dependent. As a result, a certain method of inducing hypnosis (authoritarian) might succeed when the individual was sick, but when the same person was well and relatively independent, use of this very same method might fail and another type of induction (co-operative) might be successful. Inasmuch as this theory, concerning emotional instability and its relation to hypnotic susceptibility, was reached in a pathological setting (mental hospital or medical office), the conclusion is not too surprising but should not be generalized into an all-inclusive theory. Later investigations showed that individuals without pathology of any kind could be hypnotized and that some with pathology could not; consequently this theory which likened the state of hypnosis to an abnormal mental condition has gradually died out in scientific circles, although its persistence in the popular mind accounts for many of our misconceptions today.

SLEEP

Another theory which was and still is held in scientific groups stresses the similarity between sleep and hypnosis. In regard to this particular theory, it may be said that psychologically such resemblance need not be present, and eliciting of such similarity (differences which are important are often overlooked) is only

209

the result of a particular method, and there are many in hypnotic induction. Psychologically, the individual in hypnosis, unlike the sleeping individual, can be alert and in contact with his environment. Physiologically such an individual is not necessarily similar to a sleeping individual in brain-waves, sweat response, heart rate, respiration, voluntary movements, knee-jerk, make-up of the blood, and so on. While the number of subjects on which the above differentiation is based leaves something to be desired, it appears that a subject in hypnosis is not necessarily like a sleeping subject, either physiologically or psychologically. Those physiological results that have been reported which likened the individual who is hypnotized to the individual who is asleep may result from techniques of induction which emphasize sleep. The mechanism involved is said to be the presence of some kind of inhibition (arrest of activity) which is said to be common to both. Entirely different results are obtained when in hypnotic induction the emphasis is on waking. In either case, to construct a theory which is based upon a specific method of induction is to see only a limited part of the problem. Recently a compromise theory which equates hypnosis with light sleep has been advanced.

With such limitations it might well be wondered why the theory of hypnosis which likens it to sleep has enjoyed such widespread popularity in scientific as well as non-scientific circles. The reason for this may be found in the name and research work of the internationally known Russian physiologist, Pavlov. It is not clear, however, whether he thought it was *similar* to sleep or whether he considered hypnosis the *same* as sleep. In addition, it must be remembered that Pavlov was working with animals, not human beings, and that generalization from one to the other requires considerable caution. Furthermore, his concept of inhibition (to which he likened both hypnosis and sleep) was based on responses that he found in animals by using one physiological system, salivation. Had he used more than one physiological system at a time, he would have found that his system of types, excitatory and inhibitory, did not necessarily hold for all animals, and that any one animal might conceivably be excitatory in one system (heart) and inhibitory

210

in another (salivary). Had he discovered this (instrumentation in his time was not sufficiently advanced), it is debatable whether he would have equated hypnosis with sleep via the intermediary of inhibition. It might also be argued that if sleep is the same as hypnosis, then one might legitimately expect to have people go more easily from sleep into hypnosis than from a waking state. This relationship has not been demonstrated, nor has the effect of suggestion which is known to be significant during hypnosis been shown to be active during sleep.

In summary then the reasons for equating hypnosis and sleep are varied. The findings and beliefs of Pavlov, the words used in certain methods of hypnotic induction, 'awake', 'sleep' (in waking hypnosis the terms 'awake' and 'sleep' are never used), the presence of amnesia which is generally present for dreams during ordinary sleep, and so on. That there are similarities is not debated and is obvious, but that there are important differences is also equally clear. Normal every-night sleep, hypnotically induced sleep, and hypnosis must first be described in detail before they can be equated. The fact that both sleep and hypnosis incorporate a broad range of phenomena, and may be manifested in varying degrees constitutes a stumbling-block to theory formulation.

ROLE-PLAYING

This current theory stresses the fact that a person in hypnosis acts as he believes a hypnotized person should act, as he the subject has so learned from the description and instructions given to him by the hypnotist and according to his own beliefs. These two sources, however, may yield radically different information, and when they do so it puts a strain on the theory. According to a variant of the role-playing theory, the phenomenon of anaesthesia is produced by imaginative focusing or by striving to obtain the desired condition. Such focusing or concentration on obtaining the desired end is said to heighten the possibility of producing anaesthesia, although it is not clear just how this is accomplished.

That a certain amount of role-playing takes place in hypnosis (and unfortunately is not recognized, as witness the instances purporting to show reincarnation) is very likely, but this raises the question of how far the role-playing will be carried. In physiological systems which have a voluntary component (respiration) an argument for the presence of role-playing may be made, but such an argument is not easy to make for those physiological systems which are affected by hypnosis but which have no or very little voluntary component (sweat response). When one considers that a major operation with hypnotic anaesthesia may be performed in which the patient behaves 'like a corpse throughout' or that an early infantile reflex may reappear, the concept of imaginative focusing in role-playing is not very helpful or enlightening. Supporters of a role-playing theory or some slight variant of it further state that the suggestions made to the subject are effective in an altered state of consciousness, or in an altered state of personality, or by creating circumstances suitable for the acceptance of a given suggestion. Such an elaboration again does not help our understanding of hypnosis, for it now merely paraphrases the original question from 'What is hypnosis?' to 'What is this altered state of consciousness, or personality, or what are the circumstances suitable for the acceptance of suggestion?'

If hypnosis is expectancy in the form of role-playing, what of failures to hypnotize people who are firmly convinced that they can be hypnotized, and are aware of how the hypnotized person is supposed to act? To such a question, it might be said that such individuals do not possess the required altered state of consciousness. This, however, as has been indicated, does not explain much of anything. If we were to push this theory as to why it is that only some people have and others do not possess this gift of role-playing, answers in terms of aptitudes are also encountered. Again such an answer begs the question. This particular explanation is often given when the question of why all hypnotists (who should know the role expected) are not hypnotizable. Then again, if hypnosis is role-playing, should not the experiment on muscle set (p. 97) have had a different outcome? That is, should not the group who were told that the experimenter expected positive results have given positive results; and the group who were told that the experimenter expected negative results, given negative results; and so on. It is said, in this theory, that the subject acts in such a way as to please the hypnotist. Undoubtedly some do, but undoubtedly some do not. For example, some individuals may describe their reaction to fear by saying they were 'rooted to the spot'. In all likelihood some are figuratively but some are literally. It is important to realize that such a dual reaction is possible. Role-playing (while granted it is not conscious, make-believe, or faking) deals with only one aspect of the issue. Or what of the two individuals who claimed disability, instigated a lawsuit for compensation, and yet when in hypnosis showed no sign of their claimed disability – what does this do to the theory of role-playing?

Historically, hypnosis was reported to be active and its presence was characterized by convulsions. It was only later that what we know today as passive or sleep-like hypnosis was described. The theory of role-playing would have a difficult time explaining such a change. In reading about this theory, one cannot escape the feeling that words are being played with. Needless to say, the data advanced to support this theory or any variant are taken from the lighter side of the scale measuring hypnotic depth.

HYPERSUGGESTIBILITY

The most frequently encountered statement or theory of hypnosis that is found in the psychiatric and psychological literature of today is that hypnosis is a state of hypersuggestibility. In this state everyday suggestions are said to be 'twice' as effective as in the non-hypnotic state. This figure, arrived at in an experiment concerned with muscular ability, was generalized in a fashion that the author of the experiment never intended. In addition to this detail, there are numerous other objections to this particular theory. For instance, it might be asked what kind of suggestion is being referred to: primary? secondary? indirect? prestige? non-verbal? and so on (p. 85). It has been said that the mechanism whereby suggestion becomes more effective in the hypnotic state is by a narrowing of consciousness. Consequent on this, greater attention may be focused on

213

any suggestion that is given, and this in turn is then more effective. This, however, is more a statement of *what* occurs than an explanation of just *how* it occurs. It is again difficult to explain the many cases of major surgery performed with hypnosis as a sole anaesthetic, and especially cases where suggestions of anaesthesia were *not* given and yet anaesthesia was produced, unless it is said that self-suggestion was present. What of some of the unfortunate by-products (sensory and motor disturbances) that sometimes follow a hypnotic session? Is this also self-suggestion? Interpretation of the spontaneous appearance of such difficulties after termination of the hypnotic state can only be described, according to this theory of hypersuggestion, as symptoms from whose presence the individual derives benefit and which he has therefore purposely caused to appear. One might also wonder about the non-suggested appearance of spontaneous amnesia. Such an appearance might be explained again in terms of autosuggestion in that in the induction of hypnosis by the sleep technique, the very word 'sleep' is often used, and it is generally known that forgetfulness follows sleep. Reliance upon autosuggestion to explain (away) difficult problems is too much like explaining one unknown by another; furthermore, it involves reasoning after the facts. Waking hypnosis presents a more difficult case for the interpretation of spontaneous amnesia, for here the word sleep is not used, and yet amnesia may occur – why? There are many reasons why thinking of hypnosis as suggestion is detrimental. Not only does it add confusion to scientific investigation inasmuch as there are many types of suggestion, but it lends credence to the popular misconception that implies that a person who has been hypnotized must be gullible (ch. VI).

DISSOCIATION

Interpretation of hypnosis as resulting from a dissociated state of personality is sometimes encountered at present, although it was more popular some fifty to a hundred years ago. The individual in such a dissociated state is said to act *as if* certain areas of behaviour were isolated physiologically and psychologically from the total personality of the individual. This particular theory incorporates data from the total continuum of the hypnotic scale. The mechanism by which this kind of behaviour (dissociated) is said to occur is either by inhibition, in which the brain or parts of the brain are no longer capable of reacting, or it is sometimes said that the brain may be cut off from other functioning parts, becoming thus an 'insulated subsystem'. It should be realized that the nature of this dissociative inhibition, whether it be by paralysis of certain cells in the brain, by the spread of an unknown inhibitory chemical, or by drainage (the flowing out of a hypothetical excitatory nerve fluid which leaves the brain in a state of inhibition), has not been ascertained. The deeper the hypnosis and the more extreme the psychological behaviour shown, the more inclusive are thought to be the dissociated areas of the brain. Suffice it to say that there are no known neurological data which readily support the physiological aspects of this theory. Such a theory is at present mainly a matter of inference from objectively observed psychological data.

If a hypnotized subject is required to do two things simultaneously (reading and writing), one of which has been suggested in the hypnotic state, the theory of dissociation would suggest that neither of the tasks would or should interfere with the performance of the other. Both of these acts are, according to the theory, dependent upon isolated parts of the brain and should be done *as if* done alone, and consequently the speed and accuracy of either task should not be influenced by the other. In everyday waking life such a feat would be difficult, for it is troublesome to concentrate on more than one act at a time. In practice the data from hypnotic experiments in which two acts are attempted simultaneously suggest that there is a degree of interference with each other's performance, and that dissociation, instead of acting like a barrier, as the theory would require, acts more like a filter. In short, while there is some evidence of the ability to perform both tasks simultaneously and more competently in the hypnotic than in the non-hypnotic state, there is no evidence of the ability to perform both tasks as efficiently as when each is done separately.

CONDITIONING

This theory attempts to describe hypnosis in terms of conditioning (a response given to one particular stimulus is transferred by training to a new stimulus). It states that the various phenomena of hypnosis are responses not originally given to words, but which by training have come to be elicited by these very words. Difference in ease of hypnotizing is explained in terms of ease of conditioning, but again this only raises the original question in new terms – what determines the ease of conditioning? The weakness of the theory of conditioning is that it does not explain hypnosis, for it has to assume the prior existence of some hypnosis in order for conditioning to take place! It is never clear whether it is conditioning of hypnosis, which is already present, or whether it is hypnosis produced by conditioning.

The fact that conditioning is said to occur more easily in hypnosis is sometimes adduced as evidence – but evidence of what is not clear. There are data indicating that the conditioning in hypnosis that has been reported does not subscribe to the principles deduced from non-hypnotic conditioning, but rather to the attributes of post-hypnotic suggestion. The nature of the experiment performed is important. An investigation concerning the conditioned response of dilation of the pupil of the eye, where volition is not thought to be important, would be more revealing than the reported responses of coughing where volition may play a role and where the possibility of post-hypnotic suggestion being operative is present.

The explanation of hypnosis in terms of conditioning is somewhat like trading unknowns.

MISCELLANEOUS

There are many other theories and as-it-were theories of hypnosis. Many of these are variants of the preceding theories. Some emphasize the sensual or erotic (love) aspects of being hypnotized, 'the glance of surrender', 'the submissive attitude', 'the erotic trembling', 'the coital movements', 'the expression in the eyes', and so on. In reading this material one wonders whether some projection (externalization) by the hypnotist may not be involved. Still other theories speak of the resurgence of the parent-child relationship. According to this interpretation, the question whether the parent was benevolent or despotic may indicate to the hypnotist the kind of procedure that should be used as well as the depth of hypnosis that may be obtained. If the child had been submissive to the parent, then an authoritarian or domineering approach should be used, and so on. Needless to say, this theory is purely speculative. Emotional 'sensitization' produced by sickness is thought to affect the brain in much the same way as hypnosis, and as a result the hypnotic state may, it is said, be easily produced when such a condition exists (a variant of the hysteria theory). Inasmuch as both emotional sensitization and hypnosis are not understood, such a theory is much like saying that two unknowns by virtue of their being unknown are equal to each other. The most recent theory of hypnosis speaks of it as 'concentrated relaxation'!

More recent and possibly more relevant to the data now being obtained are the theories which attempt to explain hypnosis not by any single factor (simple determinism) such as the spread of inhibition, suggestibility, or the like, although it is debatable whether these are single factors, but in terms of many many factors all cooperating to bring about the state that we know as hypnosis (multiple determinism). In all likelihood such a manifold approach is more likely to result in success, for it is realized now, more than ever, that few diseases or phenomena of behaviour are determined by any one single factor or even a few factors. We should not seek for a simple causal relationship. A is more likely a result of B, C, D, E, and F than of B alone.

MECHANISM

The physiological mechanism whereby a theory is said to work depends for its understanding on first having a full behavioural description implied by the theory itself. The picturesque statement that hypnosis allows 'the mind to slip out of gear' or that in hypnosis 'there is an opening and closing of switches' is in no way helpful. It is frequently confusing to find the terms mechanism and theory used interchangeably rather than mechanism merely being employed as an aspect of theory. In the past few years two explanations of hypnosis have appeared. One of these was entitled 'Preface to a Theory', and the other described the 'mechanism' underlying hypnosis. Both such attempts, in the writer's opinion, reflect a greater degree of humility and caution than has been shown in the past. It may be said that the presence of such qualifications as 'preface' and 'mechanism' are more consonant with the present state of the data.

Some theories try to incorporate the concept of mechanism, while others, finding it a stumbling-block, ignore it. When mechanism has been incorporated, separation of the parts of the brain and, as a consequence, their ability to function independently of each other is described. Or the mechanism which is detailed speaks of the spread of inhibition (cortical or subcortical) or the existence of circumscribed areas of excitation or inhibition in the brain. Such areas are said to be surrounded by other areas of excitation or inhibition. In addition, descriptions are given of the blocking of nerve pathways (not actually shown but based on inference), the blocking of impulses at the level of the brain, or the removing of barriers between higher and lower parts of the brain. All these and a medley of other mechanisms have been reported. As has been repeatedly emphasized, neurological observations supporting such mechanisms are lacking.

The writer's position with regard to theory-formulation in hypnosis is simply that to theorize at present is to limit. He may be accused of taking the easy way out, or, on the other hand, there may be truth in the statement that at present none of the theories is very enlightening or, and this is an important aspect of science, very predictive. This may well be a result of the attempt to find a simple relationship to account for the phenomena of hypnosis. It is believed that with the data available at present, the best procedure is to attempt to describe hypnosis by what it does rather than what it is. It is from this point of view that this book has been written. It is believed that from the accumulation of more data theories acceptable to more investigators will result.

Chapter XV

CONCLUSION

IN this book it has been said and said many times that hypnosis is neither a cure-all in therapy nor the wherewithal of research. It does, however, have its legitimate uses in both these areas – to the advantage of the patient, the therapist, and the experimentalist. In the past, as is so often the case with new applications, exaggerated claims have been made concerning the efficacy of hypnosis. Such claims did not materialize and boomeranged to the disadvantage of hypnosis; however, the false enthusiasm of former times does not appear in the present-day resurgence of interest in hypnosis. Researchwise as well as therapeutically, a more rigorous scientific procedure is to be found than was true in the past. In addition, the clinical applicability of hypnosis has been broadened. It is no longer thought of as only a substitute for chemical anaesthesia, for nowadays its use as an aid in therapy has been emphasized. It is no longer confined to the few who enter a deep hypnotic state, but extends to the many who enter a light hypnotic state. Even if one were to reduce the number of claims concerning the efficacy of hypnosis by 75 per cent and the degree of success in individual cases by a similar amount, the results would still be impressive and would indicate the therapeutic value of hypnosis. On the basis of these facts, it is the prediction of the writer that hypnosis has a foot in the door of legitimate science and is here to stay.

The writer only wishes that he could make the statement that he encountered at the end of a certain little pamphlet on hypnosis: 'There are many more larger books published on the subject, but very little can be learned from any of them, and in none is the subject so clearly explained as in this little book!'

The only fitting conclusion that can be made to a topic whose implications and applications for human behaviour have as yet been only lightly touched on is – to be continued.

SUGGESTED READING

The references given have their own references, which the reader, depending upon his interests, may choose to pursue. The findings of a number of studies whose results are reported in this book may also be found in the following citations.

Ambrose, G., and Newbold, G. *A Handbook of Medical Hypnosis.* London: Ballière, Tindall & Cox, 1956.

While this book contains many points with which this writer could take issue, it is rich in case-history material. The cases described show the range of uses to which hypnosis may be put and are clearly presented and easily understood.

Esdaile, J. *Hypnosis in Medicine and Surgery.* (Originally titled *Mesmerism in India.*) New York: Publication Society and Julian Press, 1957.

This book is of value in being, in major part, reprinted from an era of history (*circa* 1850) in which Esdaile, an English surgeon, pioneered in the use of hypnoanaesthesia. This book also contains supplemental notes by W. S. Kroger, M.D., from the present (*circa* 1957). Consequently a description of surgery and a picture of the use of hypnoanaesthesia, then and now, is made available.

Kline, M. (ed.). *Hypnodynamic Psychology.* New York: Julian Press, 1955.

This book consists of a description of hypnosis in such fields as abnormal, animal, and social. In addition descriptions are given of different techniques for the induction of hypnosis.

Le Cron, L. M. (Ed.). *Experimental Hypnosis.* New York: Macmillan, 1952.

This book consists of articles by specialists in the fields of psychiatry, obstetrics, dentistry, and psychology. Apart from applied studies, there are experimental investigations of anti-social uses, regression, automatic writing, etc. Included is a short but concise statement of the history of hypnosis.

Moss, A. A. *Hypnodontics.* New York: Dental Items of Interest Publishing Co., 1952.

This book is an easy-to-read presentation of the applications of hypnosis in dentistry. It is written with an eye to the person who has not studied or read about hypnosis and is not conversant with its applications – especially in the field of dentistry. It contains a section on case-histories of a dental nature which will be of special interest to the dentist who asserts that the proof of the pudding is in the eating. While intended primarily for dentists, it can be read profitably by anyone interested in the topic of hypnosis.

Wolberg, L. R. *Hypnoanalysis*. New York: Grune & Stratton, 1945. This book utilizes the case-history of an individual to reveal the ends which hypnosis may serve when combined with psycho-analytical procedures.

The British Journal of Medical Hypnotism, 1949 –
This journal is the official organ of the British Society of Medical Hypnotists, whose president is S. J. van Pelt, M.D., and whose editorial offices are at 4, Victoria Terrace, Kingsway, Hove 3, Sussex, England. This journal, started in 1949, consists of a number of original papers as well as reprints of more important studies that have been published in other periodicals in the field of hypnosis. While the majority of its articles are medical in nature, many are simply written and easily followed. In addition to articles concerned with medical application, there are some of a theoretical and practical nature concerning the application of hypnosis in other fields. Most important, it contains papers translated into English from foreign languages, and thus brings to the reader's attention articles which might not otherwise be available. In doing this it gives the reader some idea of the type of research going on in countries other than his own and so broadens his viewpoint about the nature of hypnosis. Its contributors are mainly physicians and dentists.

Journal of Clinical and Experimental Hypnosis. 1953–
This is a publication of the Society for Clinical and Experimental Hypnosis, whose president is R. M. Dorcus, Ph.D. Its editorial offices are at 11, Riverside Drive, New York 23, New York, U.S.A. This journal, consisting of original manuscripts only, has its beginning in the year 1953. Its contents reflect a fairly even division between the theoretical, experimental, clinical, and other applied areas of hypnosis. Its contributors are physicians, dentists, and psychologists.

INDEX

Experimental neurosis, 129
Eysenck, H., 7

Feedback, 56
Fractionation, 56
Freud, S., 121–3

Group therapy, 23
Gullibility, *see* Submissiveness
Gynaecology, 157–8

Haemorrhaging, 127, 148, 151
Hallucination, 72–3, 79, 81, 82, 110, 203, 204
Headache, 165–6
Hiccoughs, 160–1
Highway hypnosis, 201–2
Hull, C., 9, 29, 36
Hunter, I., 7
Hypers, 96–103; and memory, 99–100, 118, 125; and muscle, 96–7; and sensory acuity, 98–99, 111
Hypersuggestibility, 213–14
Hypnoanalysis, 129–31
Hypnodrama, 130
Hypnosis versus hypnotism, 13
Hypnotherapy, 117–37; criticism of, 122; direct, 125–8; forms of, 135–7; indirect, 123, 125, 128–32; symptom, 125, 133–7, 145
Hypnotizability of hypnotists, 90–1
Hysteria, 126, 172, 209

Imagination, 20, 24
Independent factors, 93–5
Induction, *see* Techniques
Insomnia, 156, 161–2
Instrumentation, 42
Insurance, 173, 196–7
Intelligence, 84
Intensification of mood, 124
International aspects, 12–13

Keller, H., 99
Kinsey, A., 108, 176
Kline, M., 102

Lancet, 27
Laws and legislation, 36, 116, 189, 193–6

Leucorrhoea, 45–6, 158
Logic, 43–4, 106, 109

Mechanical accessories, 61–2
Mechanism, 207, 210, 215, 217–218
Mental telepathy, 178–9
Mentally subnormal, 90
Mesmer, A., 22–4, 208
Messiah complex, 93, 174
Minimal clues, 55
Monoideism, 29
Mood, 47
Moral question, 104, 107–16
Muscle-reading, 179

Narcoanalysis, 131–2
Narcohypnoanalysis, 131–2
Non-susceptibility, 43, 70, 71, 83, 90, 91, 106
Non-volunteers, 91–2; *see also* Non-susceptibility

Organ selection, 46

Paralysis, of major muscles, 70–71; of minor muscles, 69–70
Passes, 22, 28, 51
Pavlov, I., 210, 211
Peptic ulcers, 164–5
Performance and potential, 96–100, 103, 139
Personality, 47–8, 83–95, 159, 212
Phobia, 126
Phrenology, 168, 209
Placebo, 140
Post-hypnotic suggestion, 55, 63, 64, 73–6, 80, 81, 82, 118, 125, 132, 156, 174, 181, 182, 201, 216
Practice, effects of, 42
Precautions, 32, 64, 78, 120, 154, 169, 172; *see also* Dangers
Prediction, 44
Prestige, 95
Psychosomatic sleep, see Dentistry
Psychotics, susceptibility of, 89–90
Publicity, 188